SMART SKETCH BOOK 8

Oogie Art's step-by-step guide to drawing portraits in charcoal and acrylic.

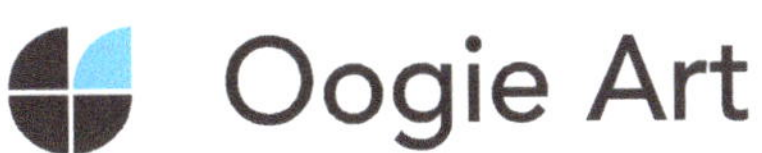

Oogie Art's SmartSketchbook™
An Expert's Guide to Portraiture in Charcoal and Acrylic
First Edition, Copyright © 2015

Produced and Edited by
Oogie Art
New York, NY

Directed by
Wook Choi

Assistant Directed by
Clara Lu

Drawings by
Jee Hwang

Tips by
Wook Choi

Published and Distributed by
Oogie Publishing House
New York, NY
www.oogiepublishinghouse.com
(212) 714-1011

ISBN 978-0-9855809-9-5
Printed in the United States

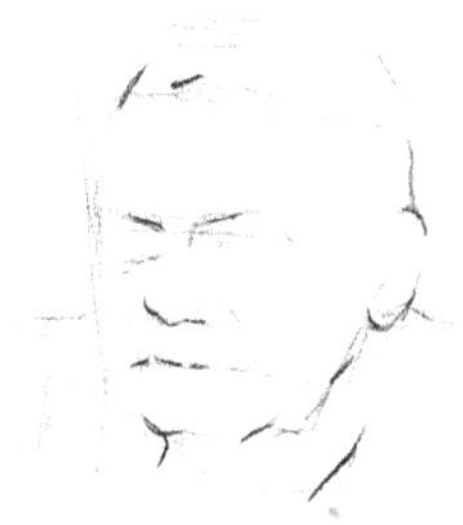
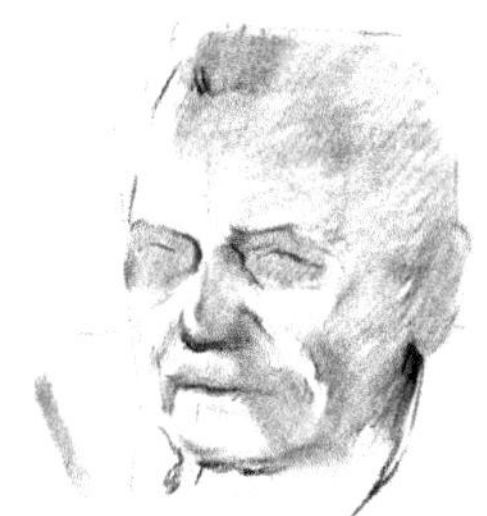
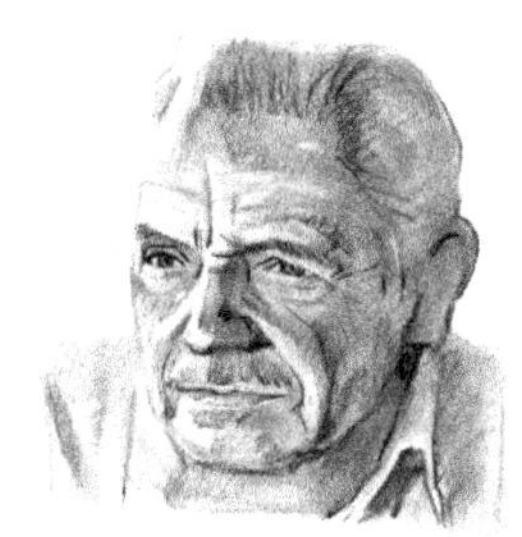
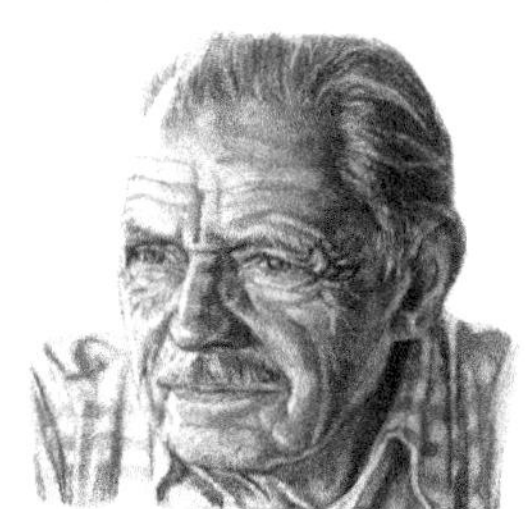

CONTENTS

Introduction to Portraiture

Portraiture is a very important genre in art dating back centuries into our history. Portraying emotion is key to a successful portrait, so knowing the underlying structure of the muscles and bones of the face will make it easier to figure out the shadows and forms of the face. Also keep in mind that the general shape of the head is spherical.

Gaze is another important aspect to consider about portraiture. A portrait's gaze informs the viewer of your piece on where to look. A portrait looking straight at the viewer creates a strong direct feeling to your drawing, while looking away makes a less direct feeling.

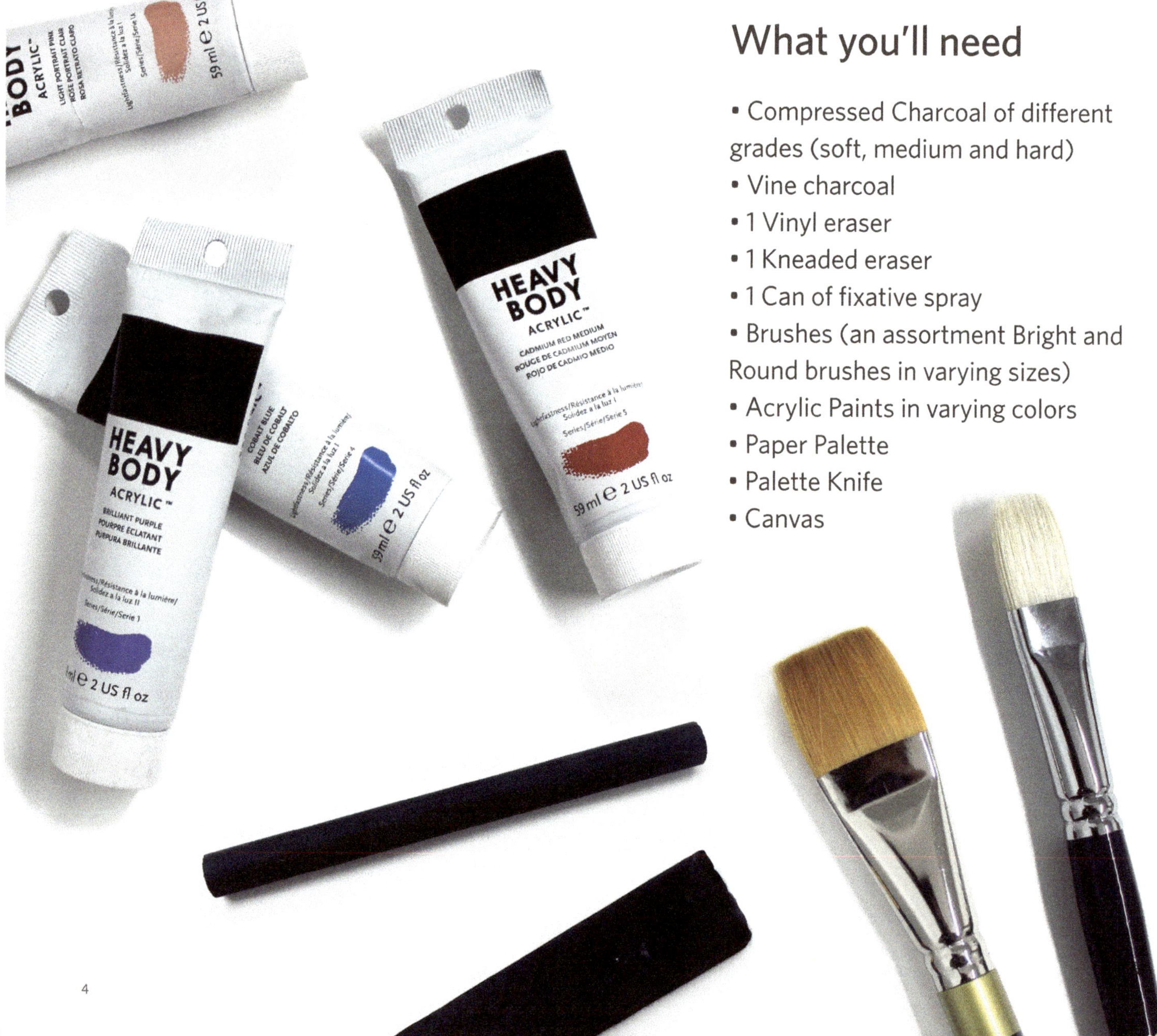

What you'll need

- Compressed Charcoal of different grades (soft, medium and hard)
- Vine charcoal
- 1 Vinyl eraser
- 1 Kneaded eraser
- 1 Can of fixative spray
- Brushes (an assortment Bright and Round brushes in varying sizes)
- Acrylic Paints in varying colors
- Paper Palette
- Palette Knife
- Canvas

It can be very daunting for the beginning artist to start drawing a face. One of the most important things to remember is where your features (eyes, nose, and mouth) are positioned. Eyes are positioned right in the middle of the head. The nose ends at the midpoint between the chin and the eyes, while the mouth is halfway between the nose and chin. Another important aspect that many artists ignore are the planes of the face. The underlying structure of the skull and muscles determine the shape of our faces.

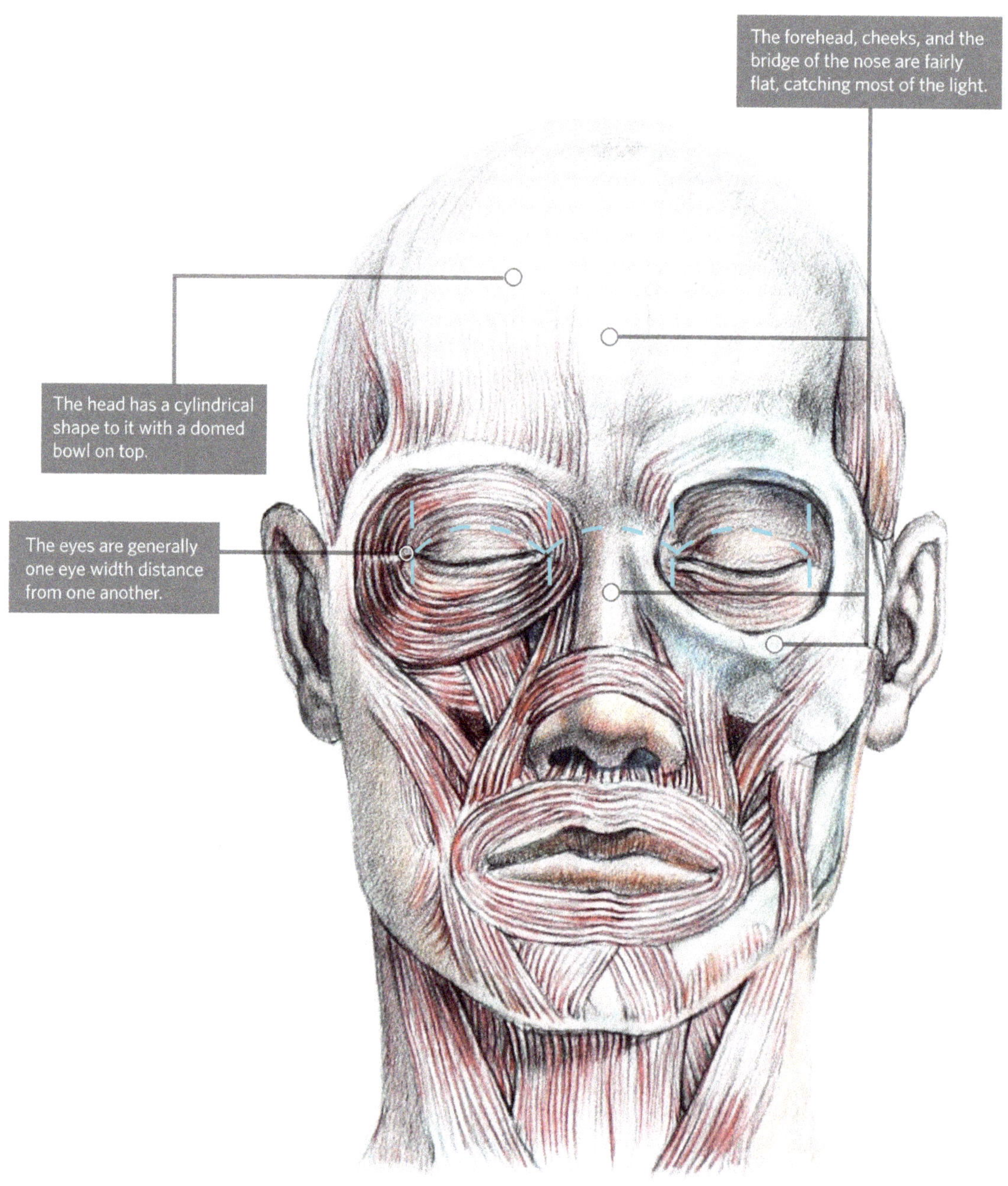

Now try drawing the face anatomy yourself.

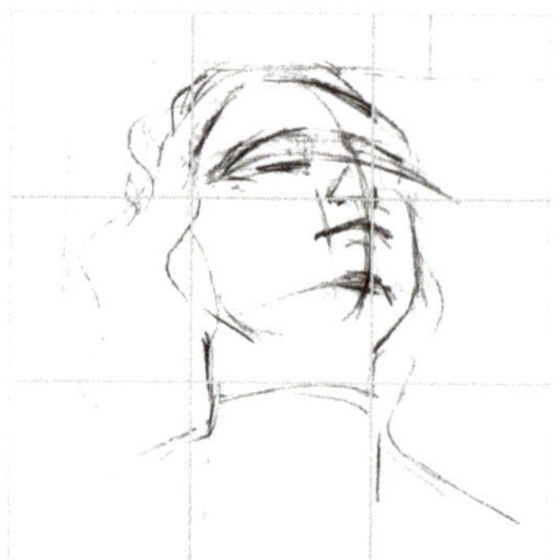

After marking the middle guideline, place the major features' positions, like eyes, nose, and mouth. Then block in the values.

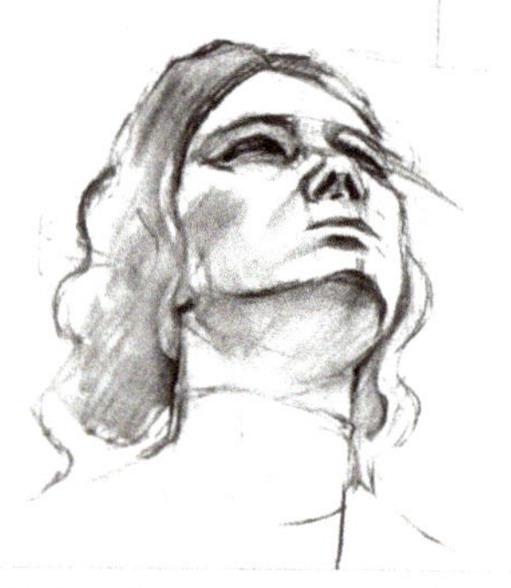

Think of the general sense of volume of the face to help smooth out the dark tones. Since the head is a bit tilted, both sides of the head should be darker, while the highlights should be directed to the parts of the head pointing to the shoulder.

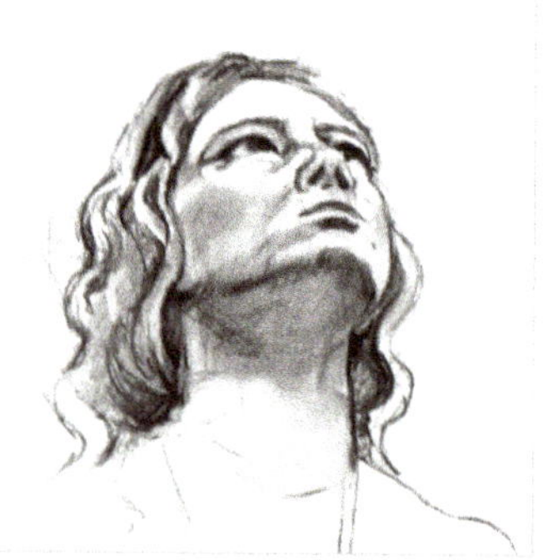

Add more detail in the shapes of the eyes, nose, and mouth. Add volume while drawing the hair.

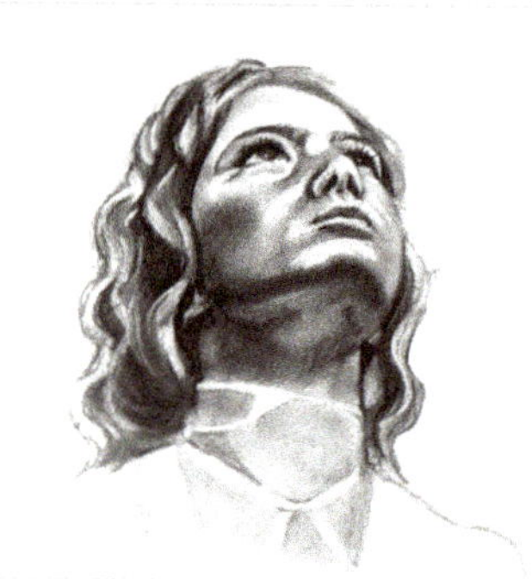

Go back over the face, adding more detail and deepening the shadows and highlights. Define the wrinkles in the clothing to finish the drawing.

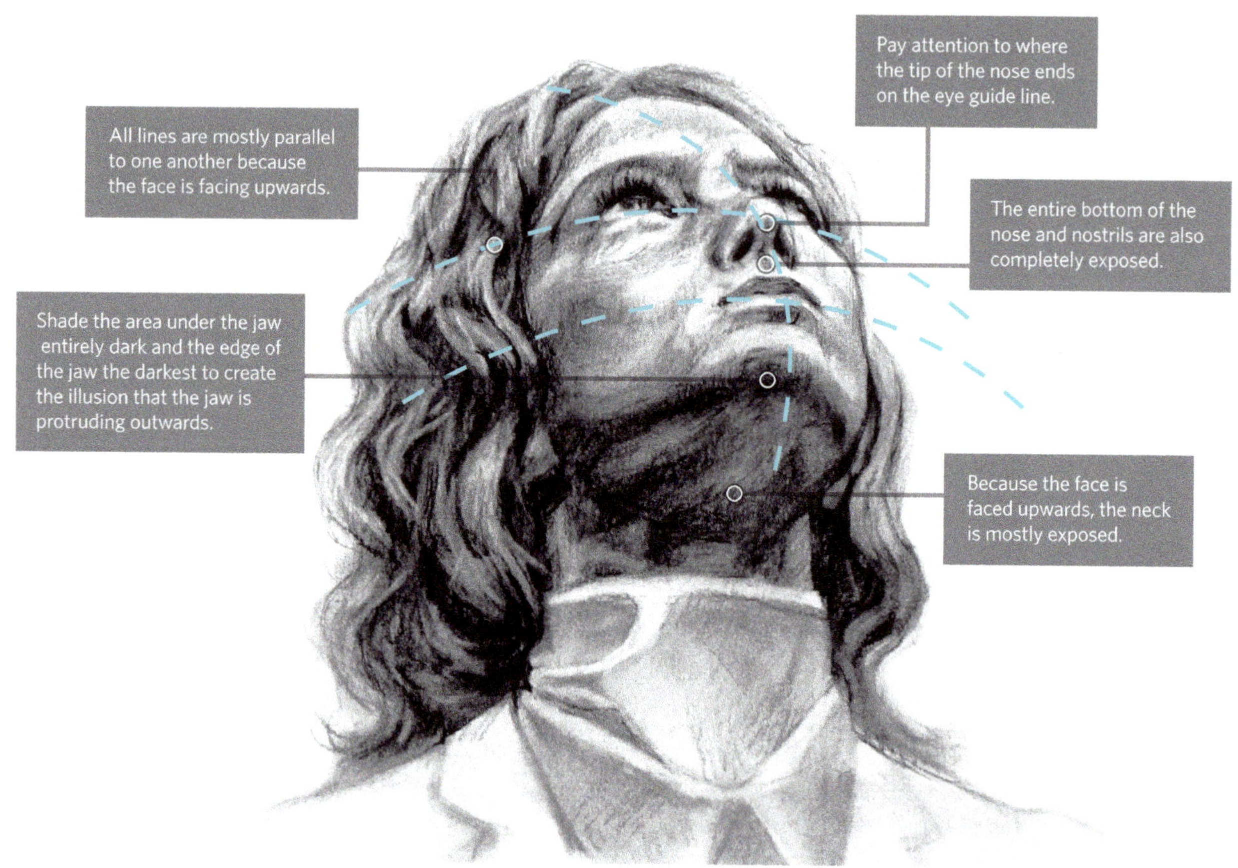

Now try drawing the portrait of the person looking up.

Now that you have practiced how to draw a face looking up in charcoal following a step-by-step tutorial, use the page on the right to try and draw from life. You can draw from the picture below, use a mirror, or ask a friend to sit for you and try different variations of compositions.

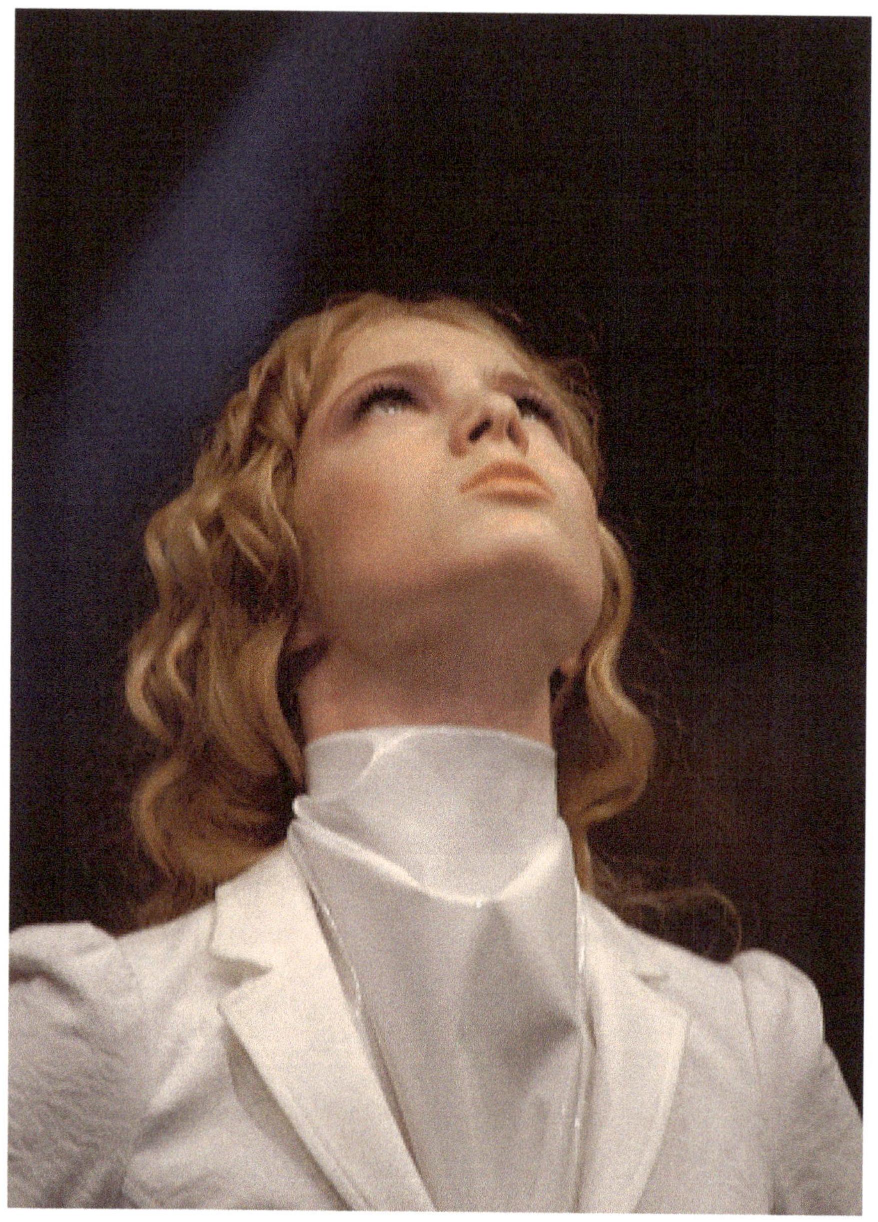

Now try drawing the portrait of the person looking up without using the grid.

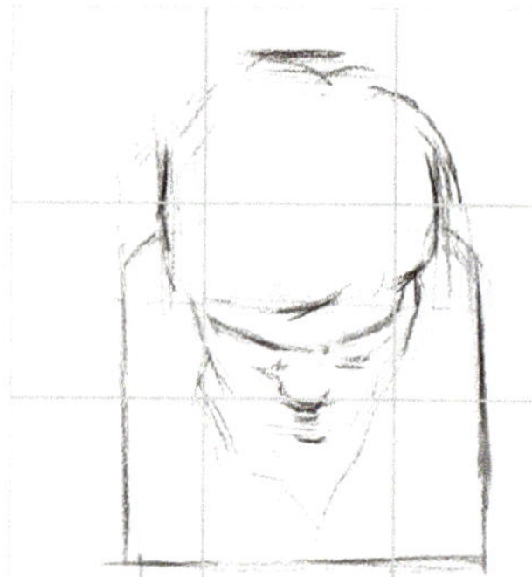

After marking the middle guideline, place the major features' positions, like eyes, nose, and mouth.

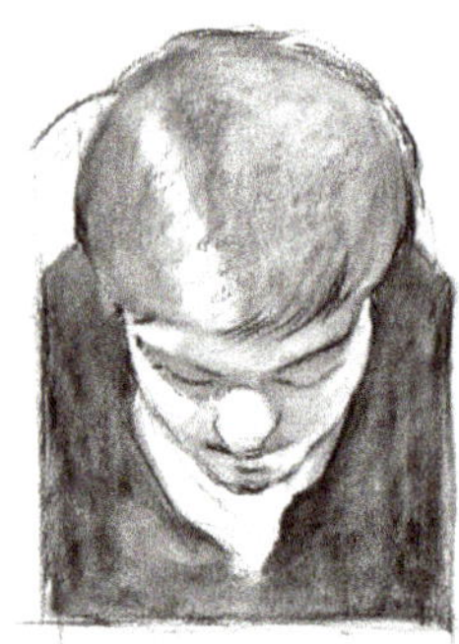

Think of the general sense of volume of the face to help smooth out the dark tones. Since the head is a bit tilted, both sides of the head should be darker, while the highlights should be directed to the parts of the head pointing to the shoulder.

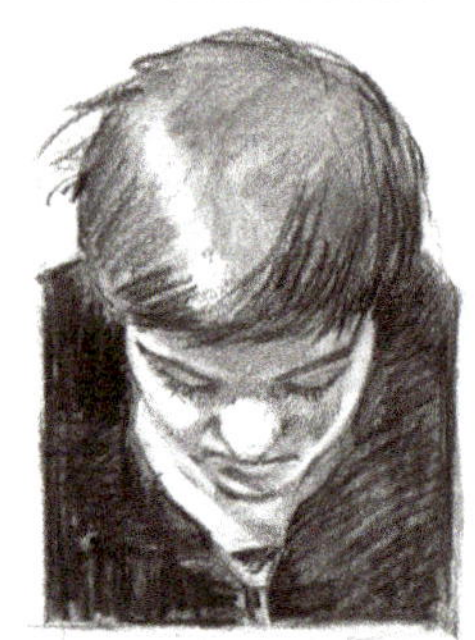

Add more detail in the shapes of the eyes, nose, and mouth. Add volume while drawing the hair.

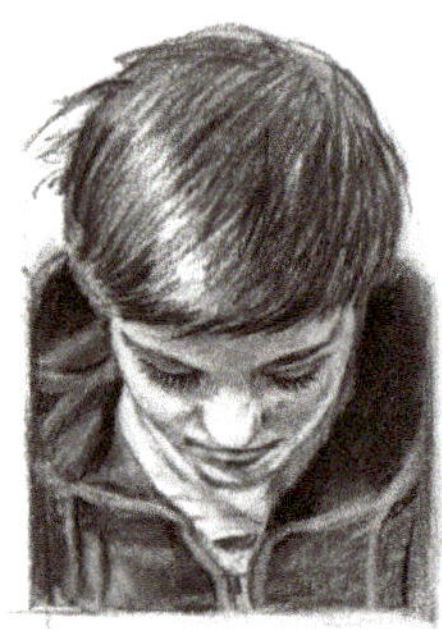

Go back over the face, adding more detail and deepening the shadows and highlights. Define the wrinkles in the clothing to finish the drawing.

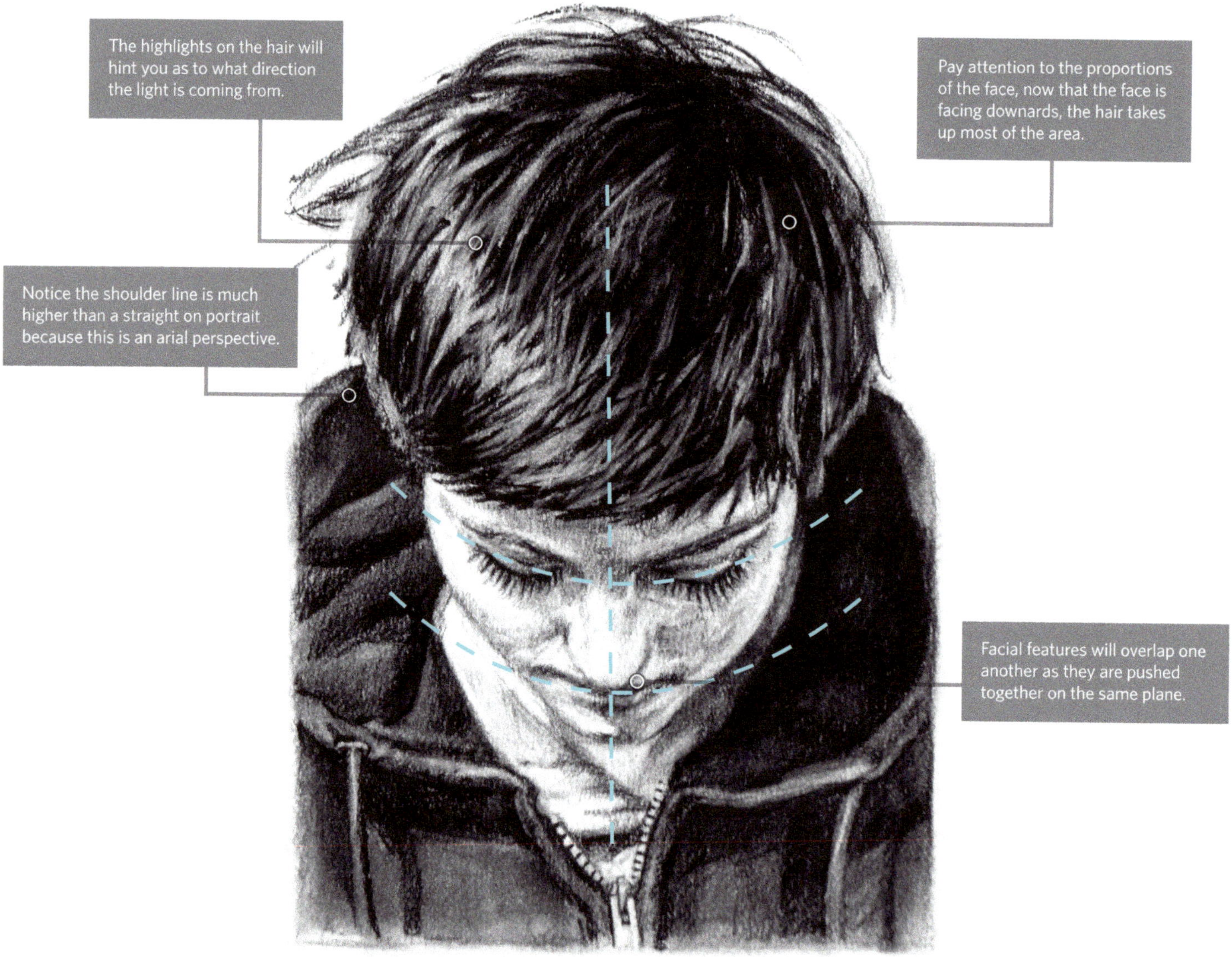

The highlights on the hair will hint you as to what direction the light is coming from.

Pay attention to the proportions of the face, now that the face is facing downwards, the hair takes up most of the area.

Notice the shoulder line is much higher than a straight on portrait because this is an arial perspective.

Facial features will overlap one another as they are pushed together on the same plane.

Now try drawing a portrait of the person looking down.

Now that you have practiced how to draw a face looking down in charcoal following a step-by-step tutorial, use the page on the right to try and draw from life. You can draw from the picture below, use a mirror, or ask a friend to sit for you and try different variations of compositions.

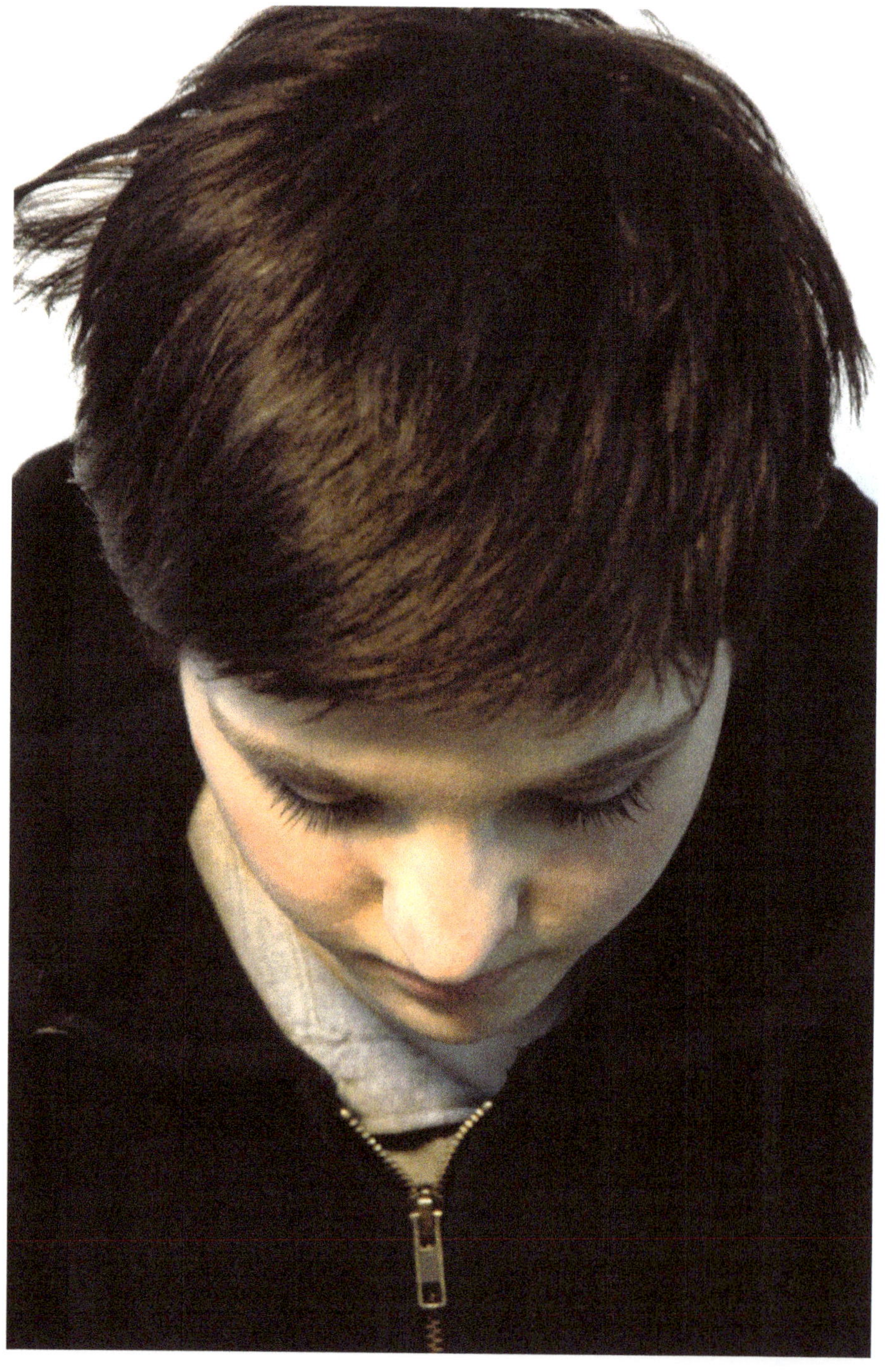

Now try drawing a portrait of the person looking down without using the grid.

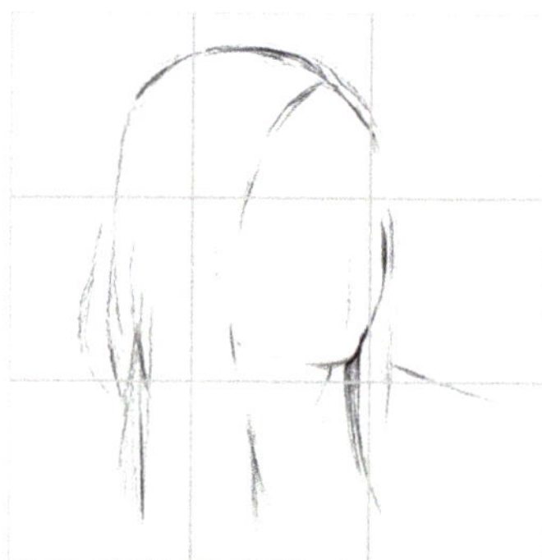

After marking the middle guideline, place the major features' positions, like eyes, nose, and mouth. Then block in the values.

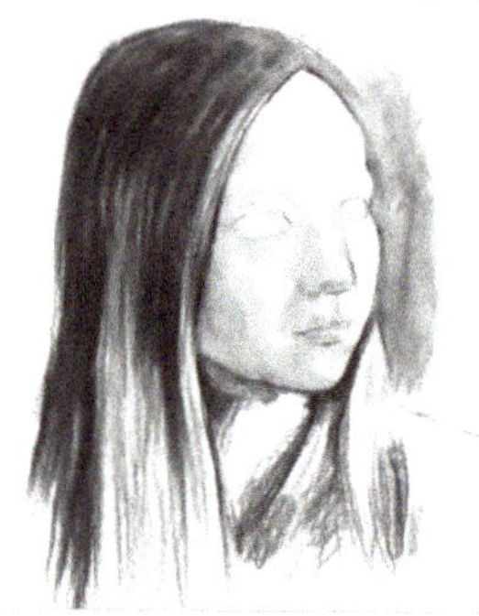

Think of the general sense of volume of the face to help smooth out the dark tones.

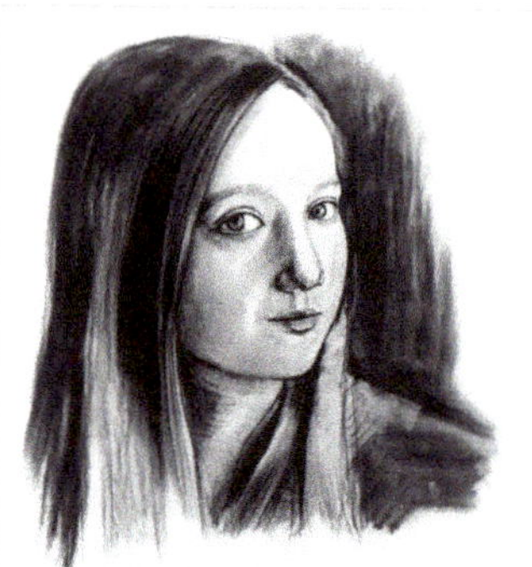

Pay attention to the different facial expressions. The forms and volumes of the cheekbones should be accurately placed.

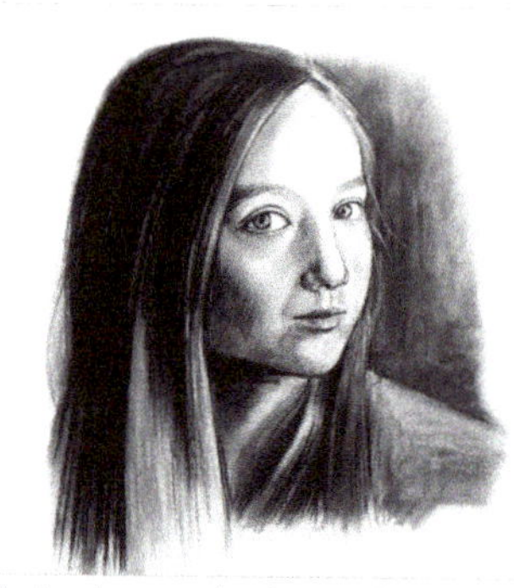

Go back over the face, adding more detail, deepening shadows, and lightening highlights, and define the wrinkles in the clothing to finish the drawing.

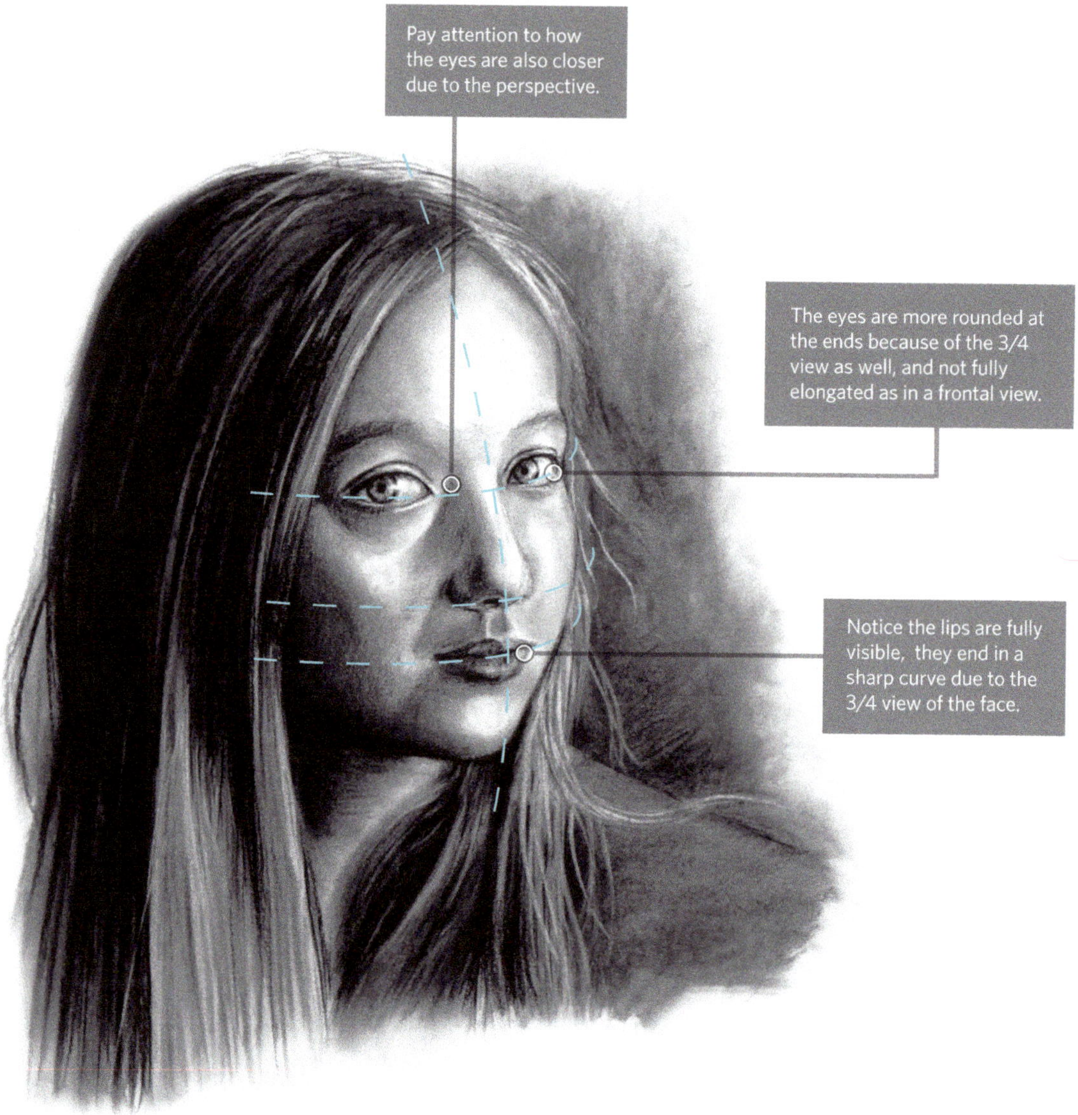

Pay attention to how the eyes are also closer due to the perspective.

The eyes are more rounded at the ends because of the 3/4 view as well, and not fully elongated as in a frontal view.

Notice the lips are fully visible, they end in a sharp curve due to the 3/4 view of the face.

Now try drawing a portrait of the young girl in a 3/4 view.

Now that you have practiced how to draw a young girl in charcoal following a step-by-step tutorial, use the page on the right to try and draw from life. You can draw from the picture below, use a mirror, or ask a friend to sit for you and try different variations of compositions.

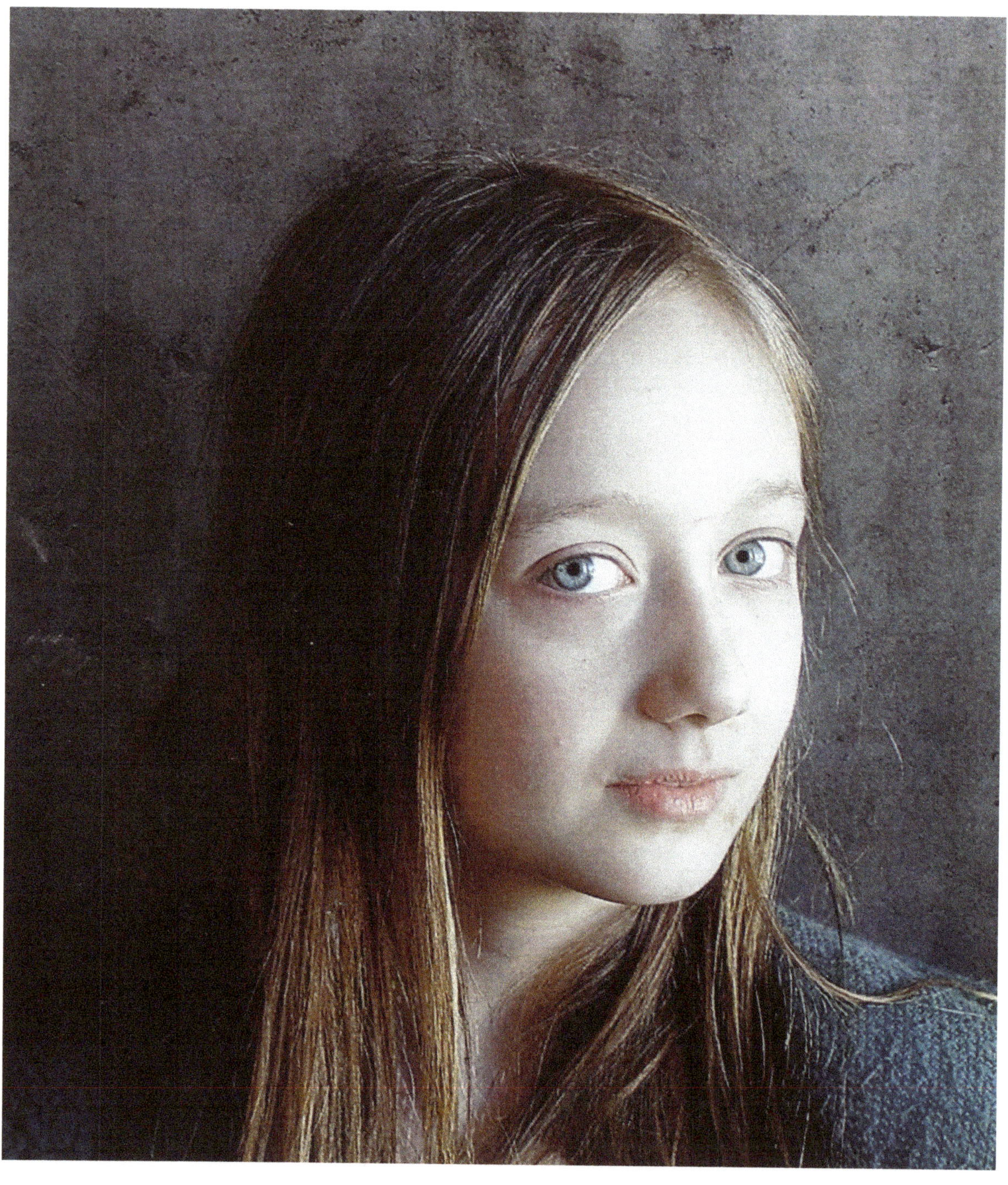

Now try drawing the girl in 3/4 view without using the grid.

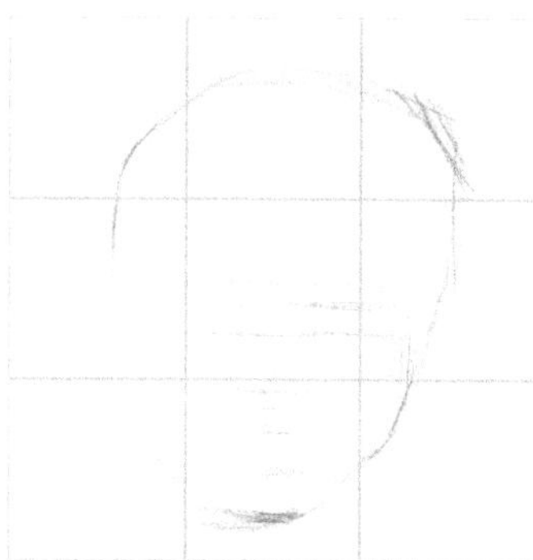

After marking the middle guideline, place the major features' positions, like eyes, nose, and mouth. Then block in the values.

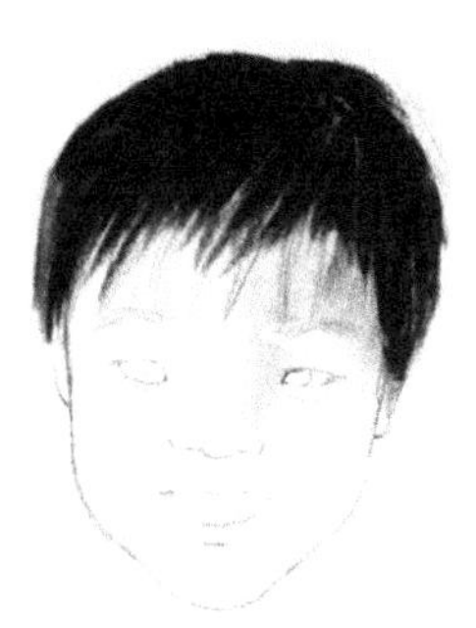

Think of the general sense of volume of the face to help smooth out the dark tones.

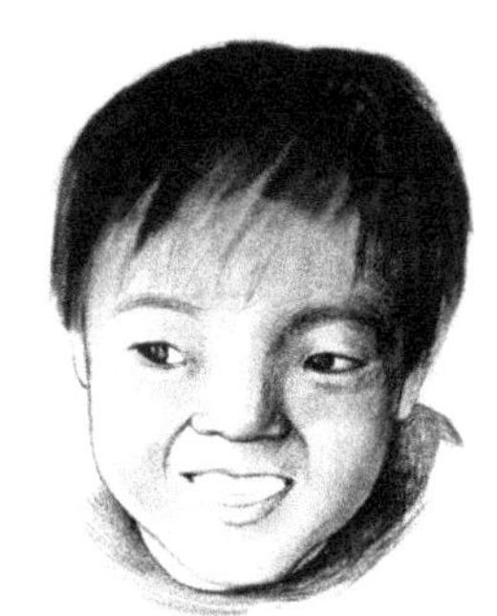

Pay attention to the different facial expressions. The forms and volumes of the cheekbones should be accurately placed.

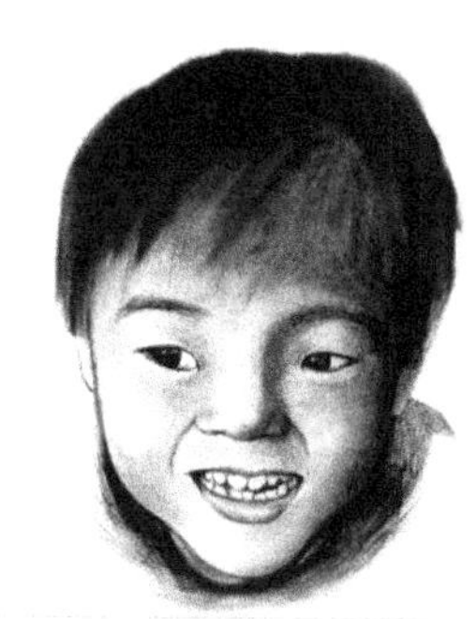

Go back over the face, adding more detail, deepening shadows, and lightening highlights, and define the wrinkles in the clothing and face to finish the drawing.

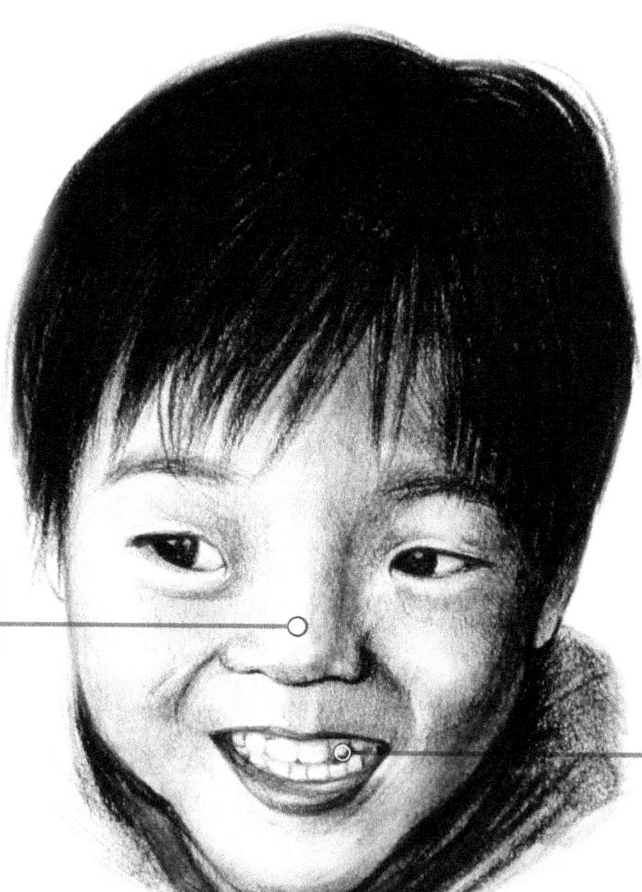

Children generally have large facial features in relation to the rest of their face.

Don't make the teeth too prominent, lightly shade the shadows in otherwise the teeth will look frightening.

Now try drawing the baby yourself.

Now that you have practiced how to draw a baby in charcoal following a step-by-step tutorial, use the page on the right to try and draw from life. You can draw from the picture below, use a mirror, or ask a friend to sit for you and try different variations of compositions.

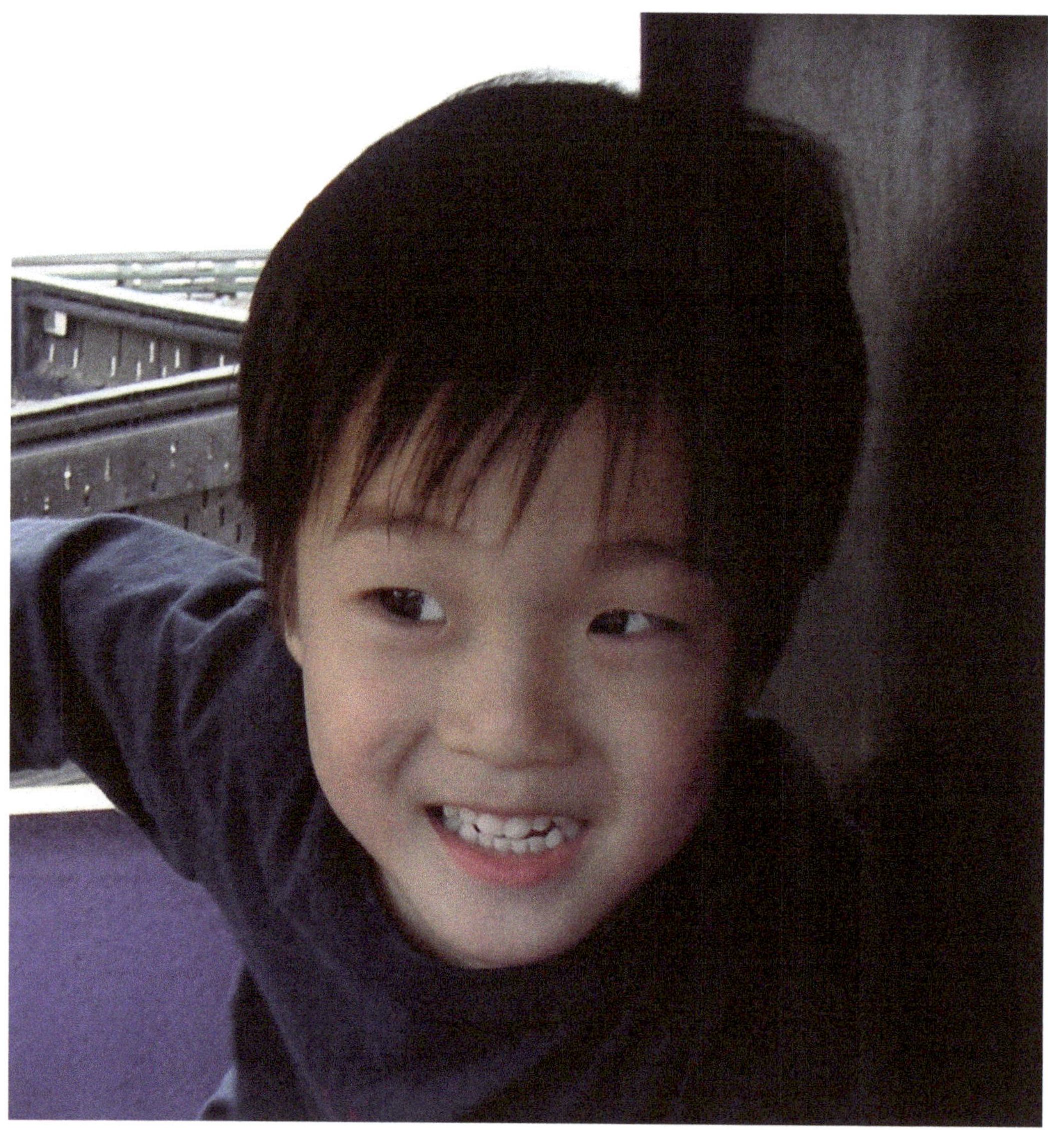

Now try drawing the baby yourself without the grid.

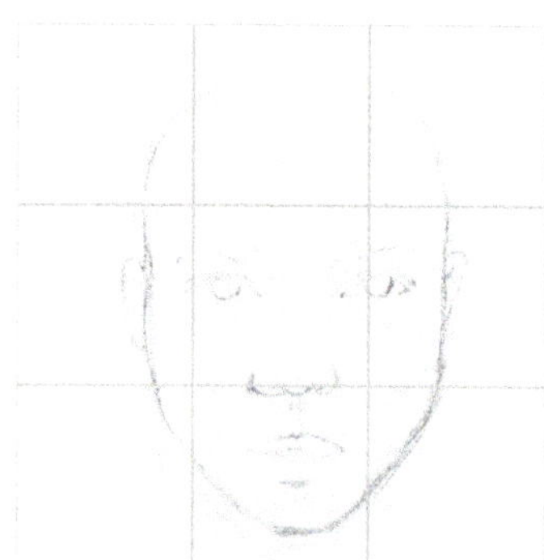

Draw the general features of the face in pencil.

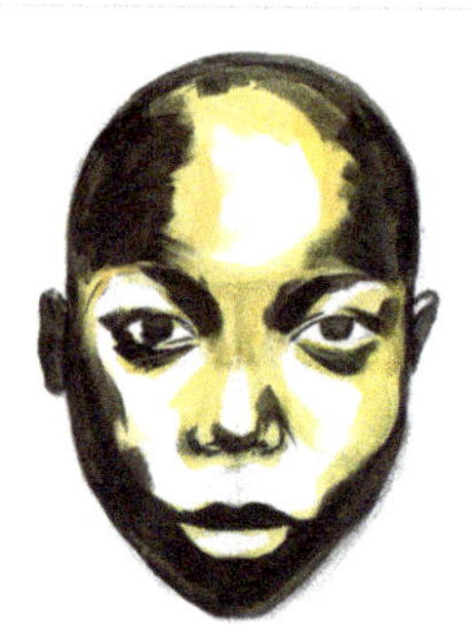

Using a light yellow and a mixture of green and red, add highlight to give volume to the parts of the face.

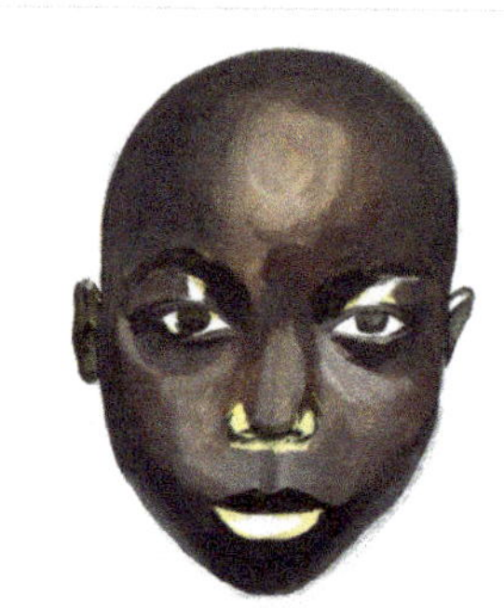

The shadows in the forms and volumes of the cheekbones should be accurately placed by observing the different facial expressions carefully by using the color brown.

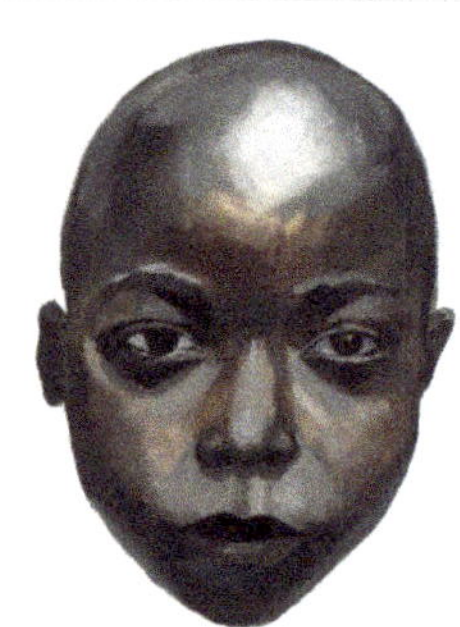

Thoroughly go back over the face with middle tone browns, and when finishing the painting, make sure to pay attention to the general volume changes throughout the face.

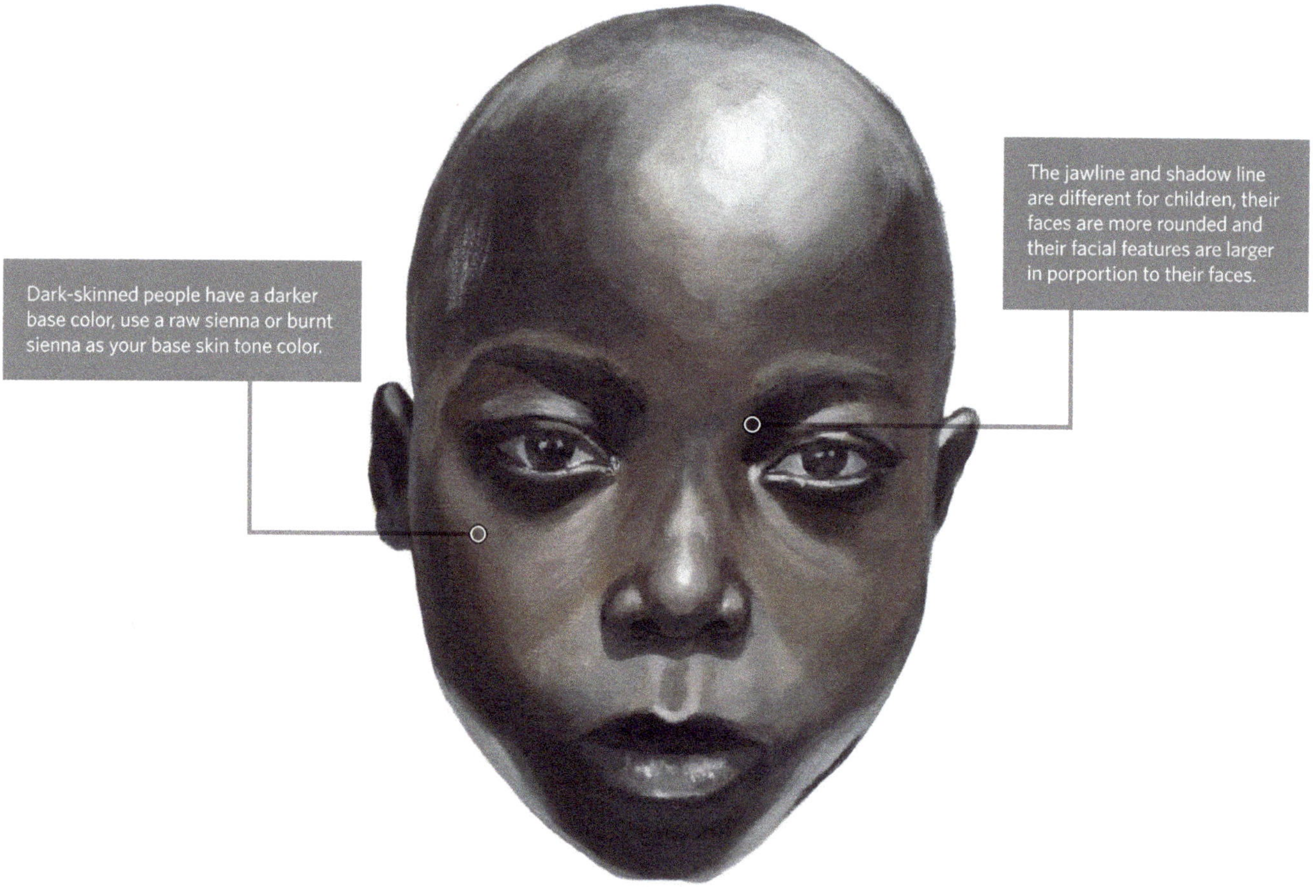

The jawline and shadow line are different for children, their faces are more rounded and their facial features are larger in porportion to their faces.

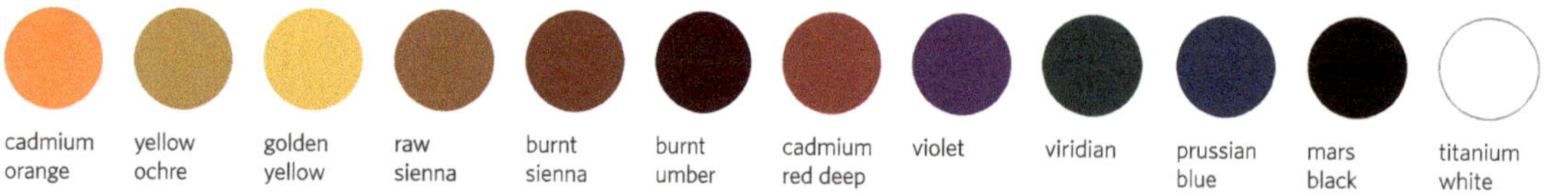

Dark-skinned people have a darker base color, use a raw sienna or burnt sienna as your base skin tone color.

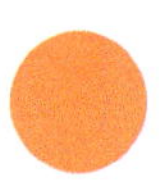
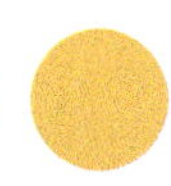
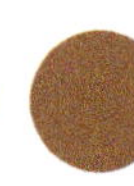

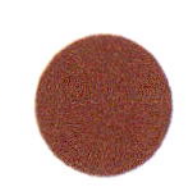
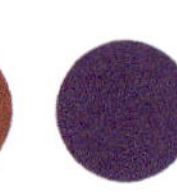
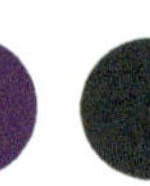
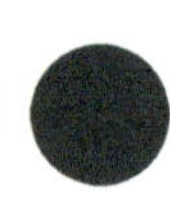

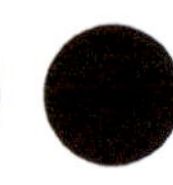

cadmium orange · yellow ochre · golden yellow · raw sienna · burnt sienna · burnt umber · cadmium red deep · violet · viridian · prussian blue · mars black · titanium white

Now try painting the child yourself.

Now that you have practiced how to paint a child in acrylic following a step-by-step tutorial, use the page on the right to try and draw from life. You can draw from the picture below, use a mirror, or ask a friend to sit for you and try different variations of compositions.

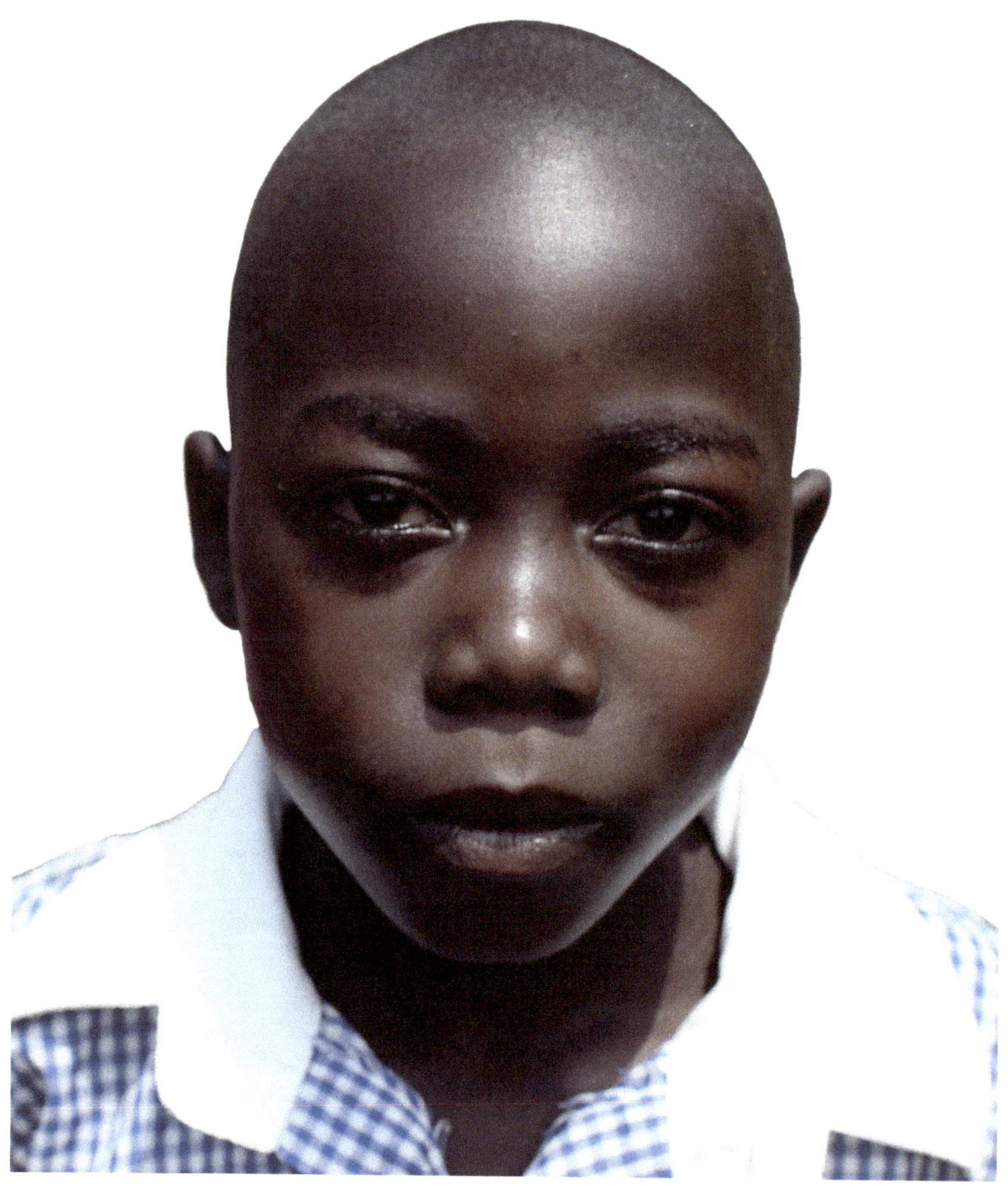

CHILD IN ACRYLIC: PRACTICE II

Now try painting the child yourself.

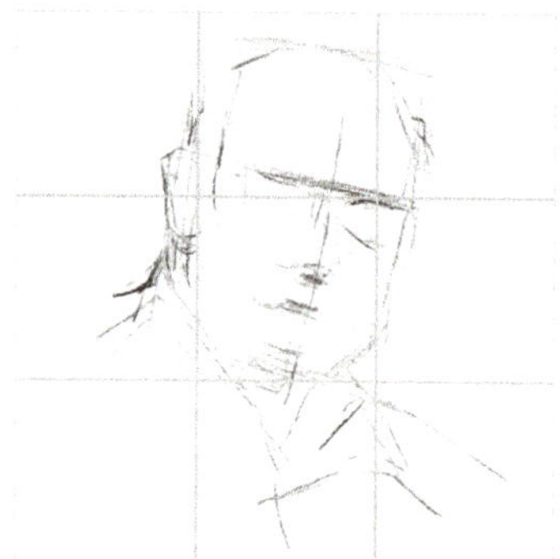

After marking the middle guideline, place the major features' positions, like eyes, nose, and mouth. Then block in the values.

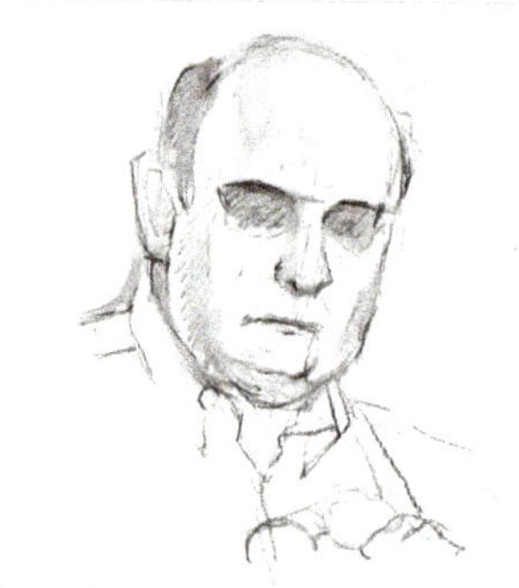

Think of the general sense of volume of the face to help smooth out the dark tones.

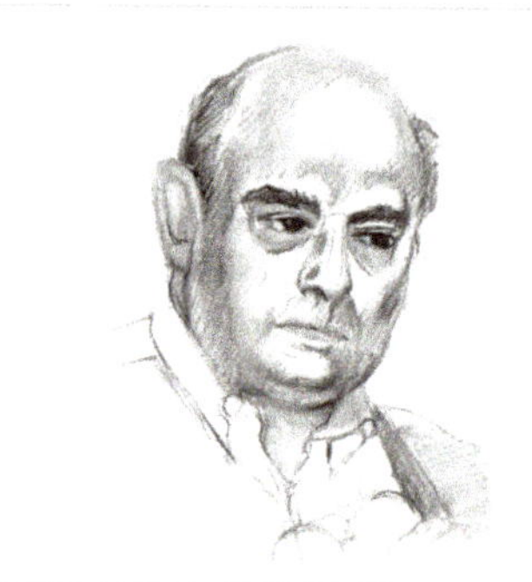

Pay attention to the different facial expressions. The forms and volumes of the cheekbones should be accurately placed.

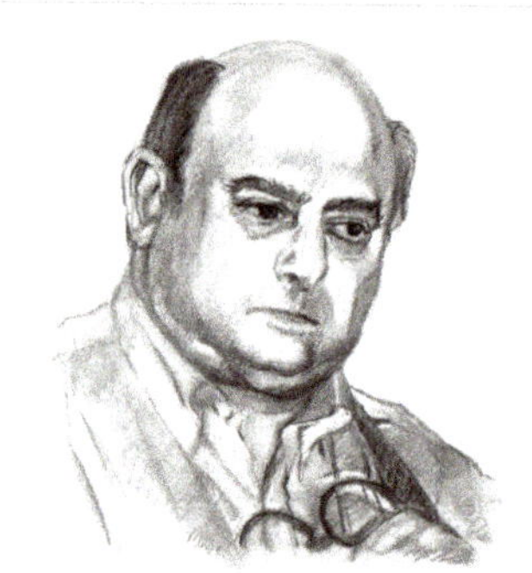

Go back over the face, adding more detail, deepening shadows, and lightening highlights, and define the wrinkles in the clothing to finish the drawing.

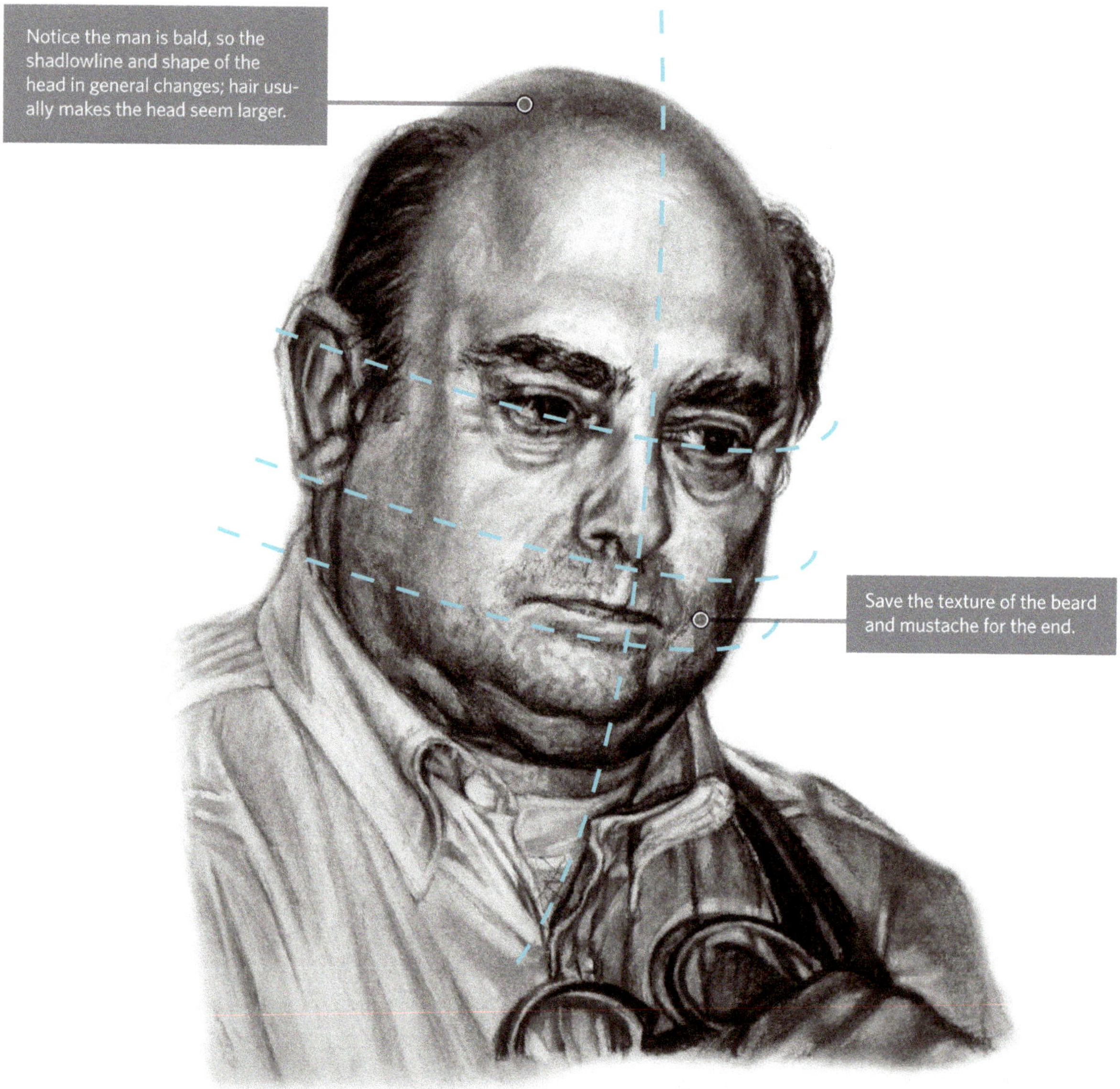

Notice the man is bald, so the shadowline and shape of the head in general changes; hair usually makes the head seem larger.

Save the texture of the beard and mustache for the end.

Now try drawing the middle aged man yourself.

Now that you have practiced how to draw a middle aged man in charcoal following a step-by-step tutorial, use the page on the right to try and draw from life. You can draw from the picture below, use a mirror, or ask a friend to sit for you and try different variations of compositions.

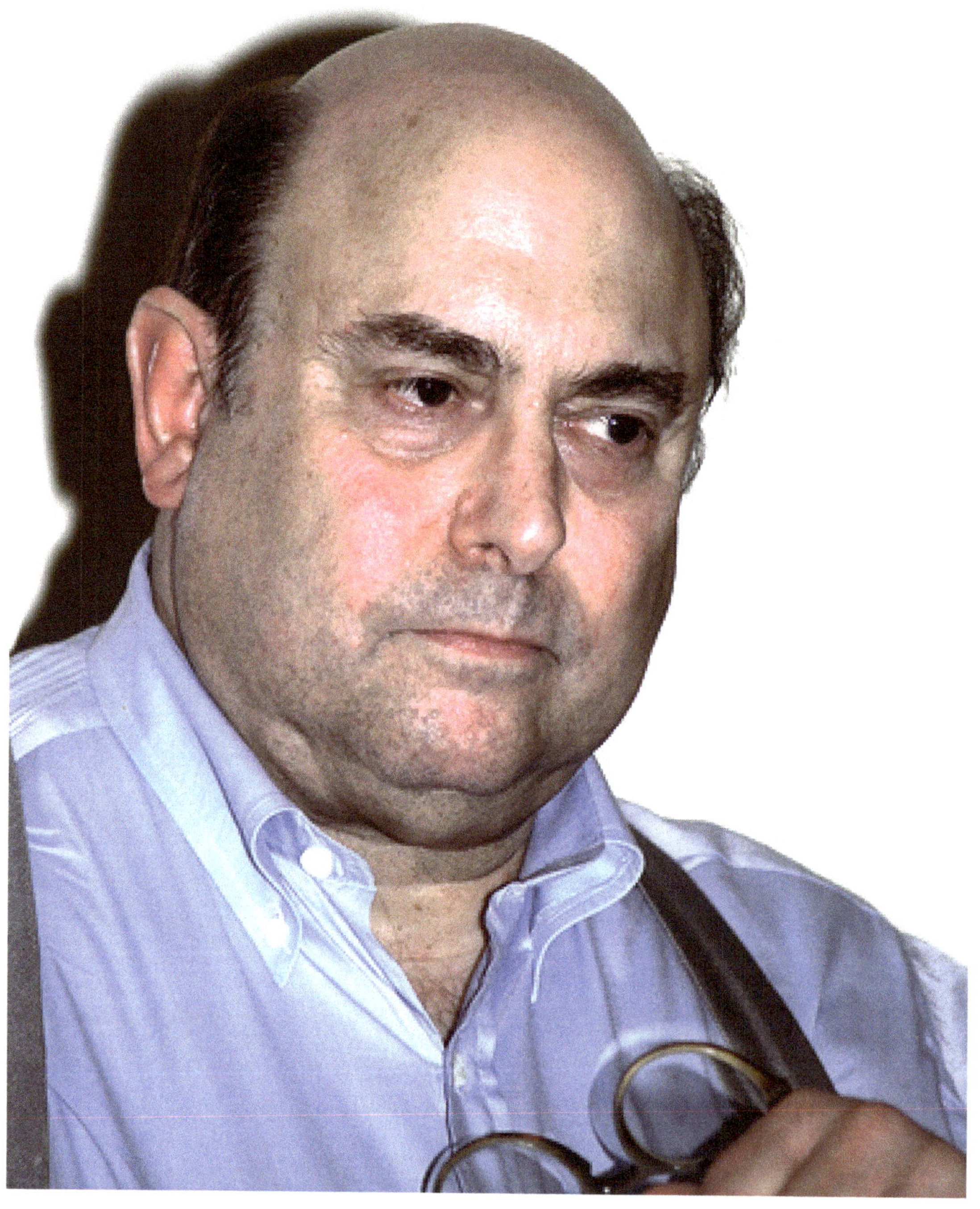

Now try drawing the middle aged man yourself without the grid.

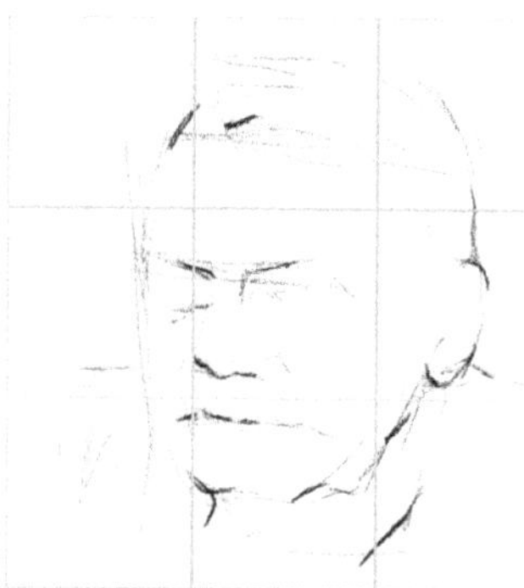

After marking the middle guideline, place the major features' positions, like eyes, nose, and mouth. Then block in the values.

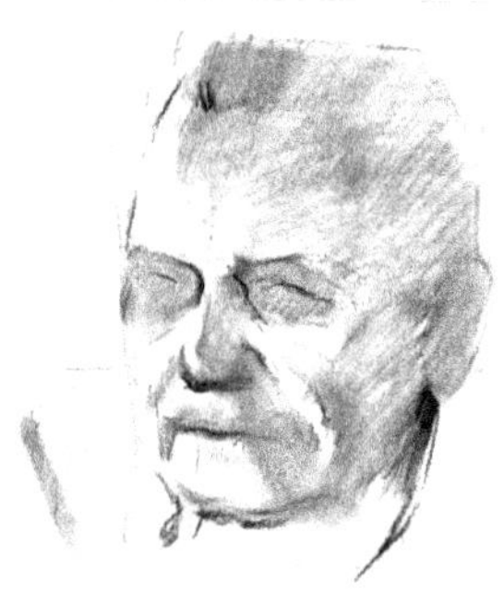

Think of the general sense of volume of the face to help smooth out the dark tones.

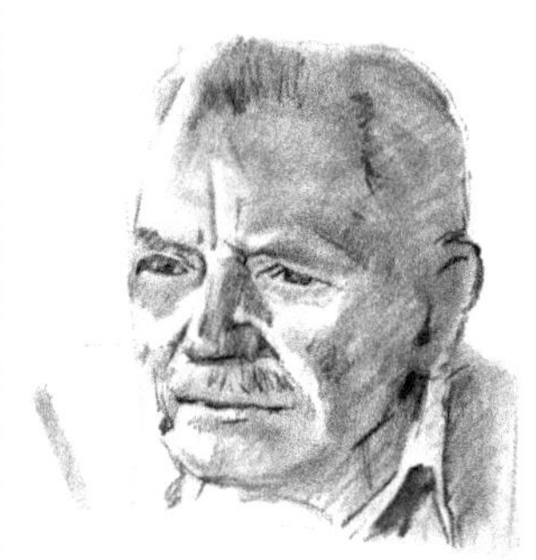

Pay attention to the different facial expressions. The forms and volumes of the cheekbones should be accurately placed.

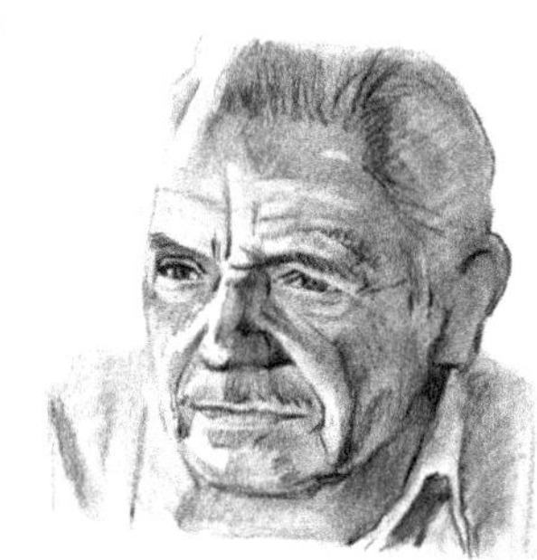

Go back over the face, adding more detail, deepening shadows, and lightening highlights, and define the wrinkles in the clothing and face to finish the drawing.

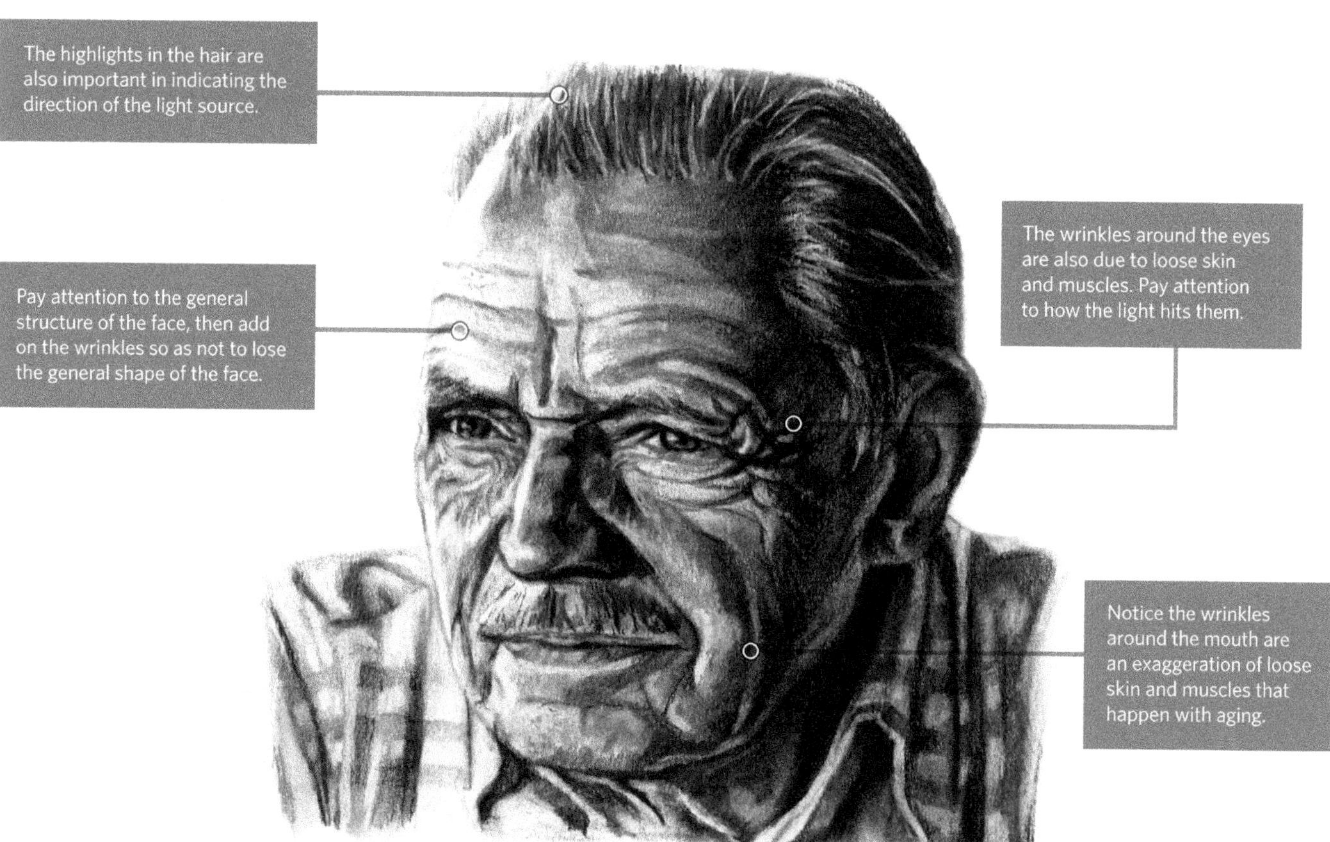

The highlights in the hair are also important in indicating the direction of the light source.

Pay attention to the general structure of the face, then add on the wrinkles so as not to lose the general shape of the face.

The wrinkles around the eyes are also due to loose skin and muscles. Pay attention to how the light hits them.

Notice the wrinkles around the mouth are an exaggeration of loose skin and muscles that happen with aging.

Now try drawing the elderly man yourself.

Now that you have practiced how to draw an elderly man in charcoal following a step-by-step tutorial, use the page on the right to try and draw from life. You can draw from the picture below, use a mirror, or ask a friend to sit for you and try different variations of compositions.

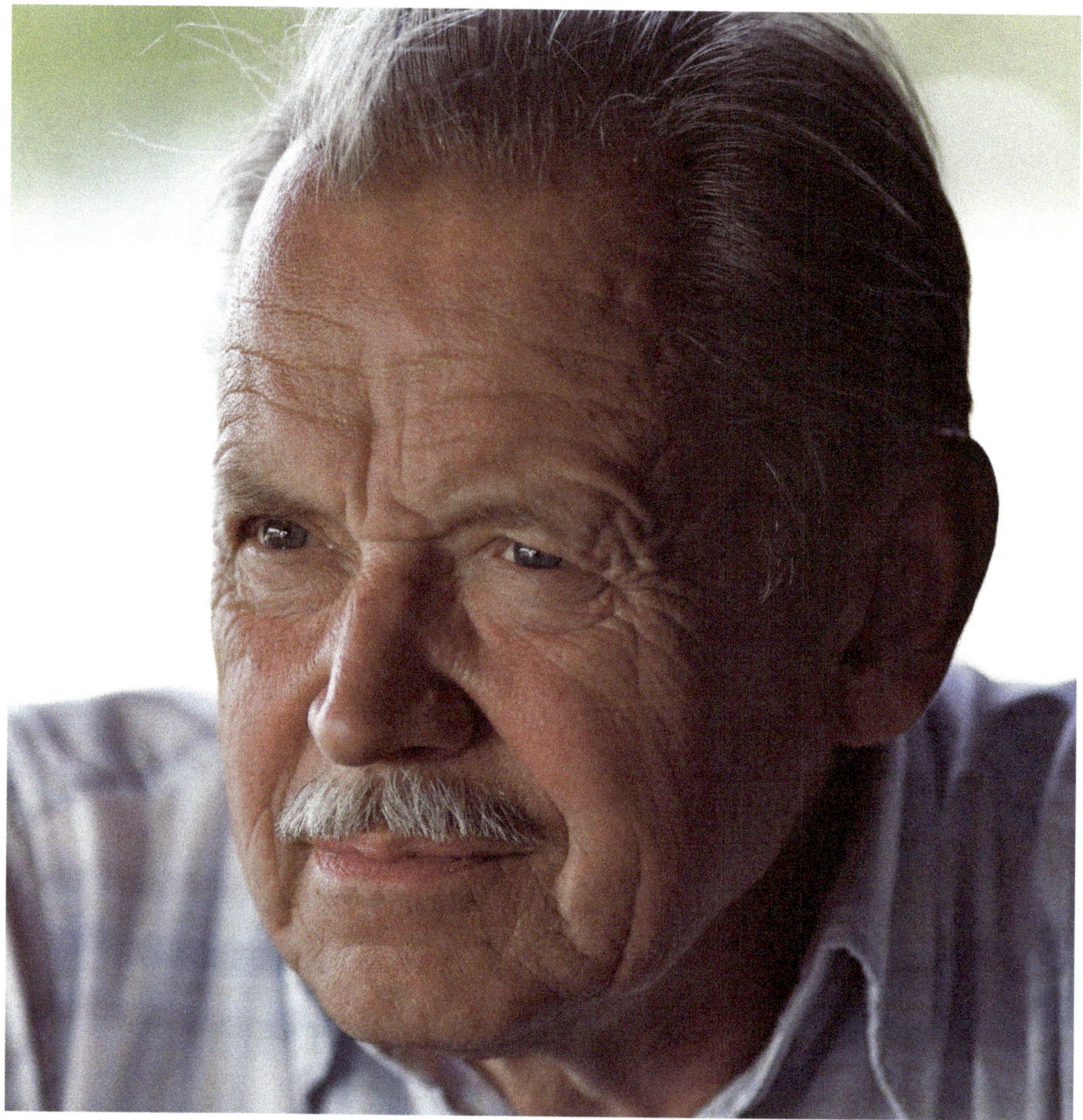

Now try drawing the elder man yourself without the grid.

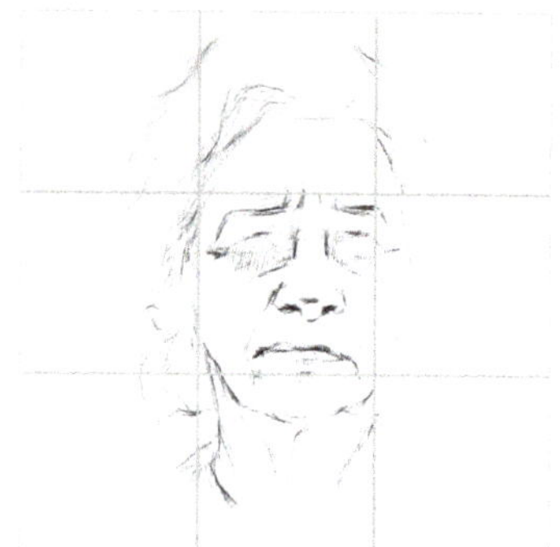

After marking the middle guideline, place the major features' positions, like eyes, nose, and mouth. Then block in the values.

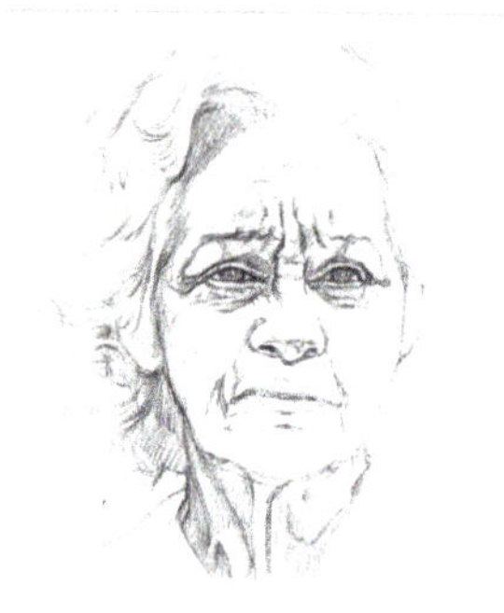

Think of the general sense of volume of the face to help smooth out the dark tones.

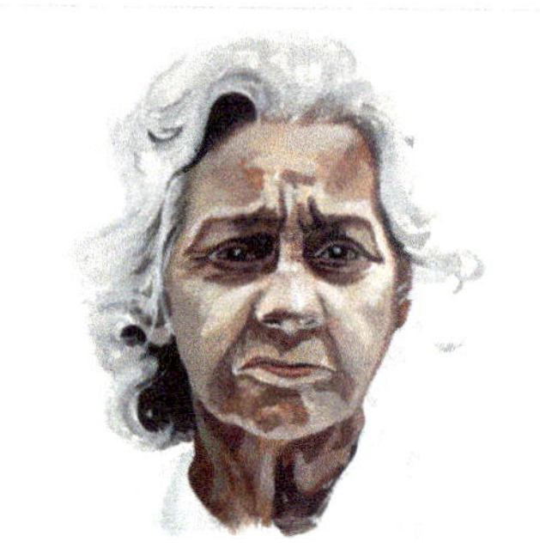

Pay attention to the different facial expressions. The forms and volumes of the cheekbones should be accurately placed.

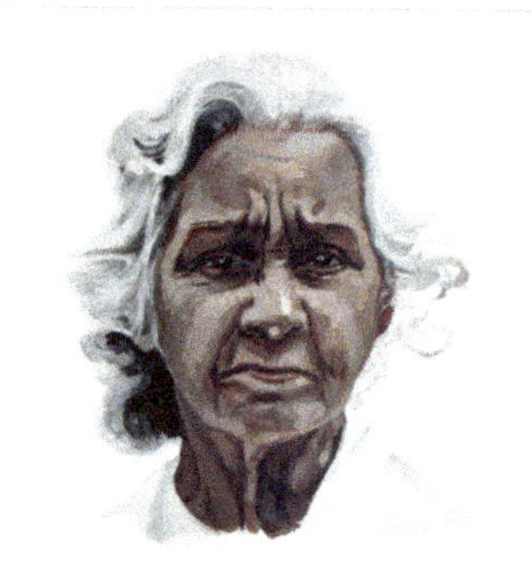

Go back over the face, adding more detail, deepening shadows, and lightening highlights, and define the wrinkles in the clothing and face to finish the drawing.

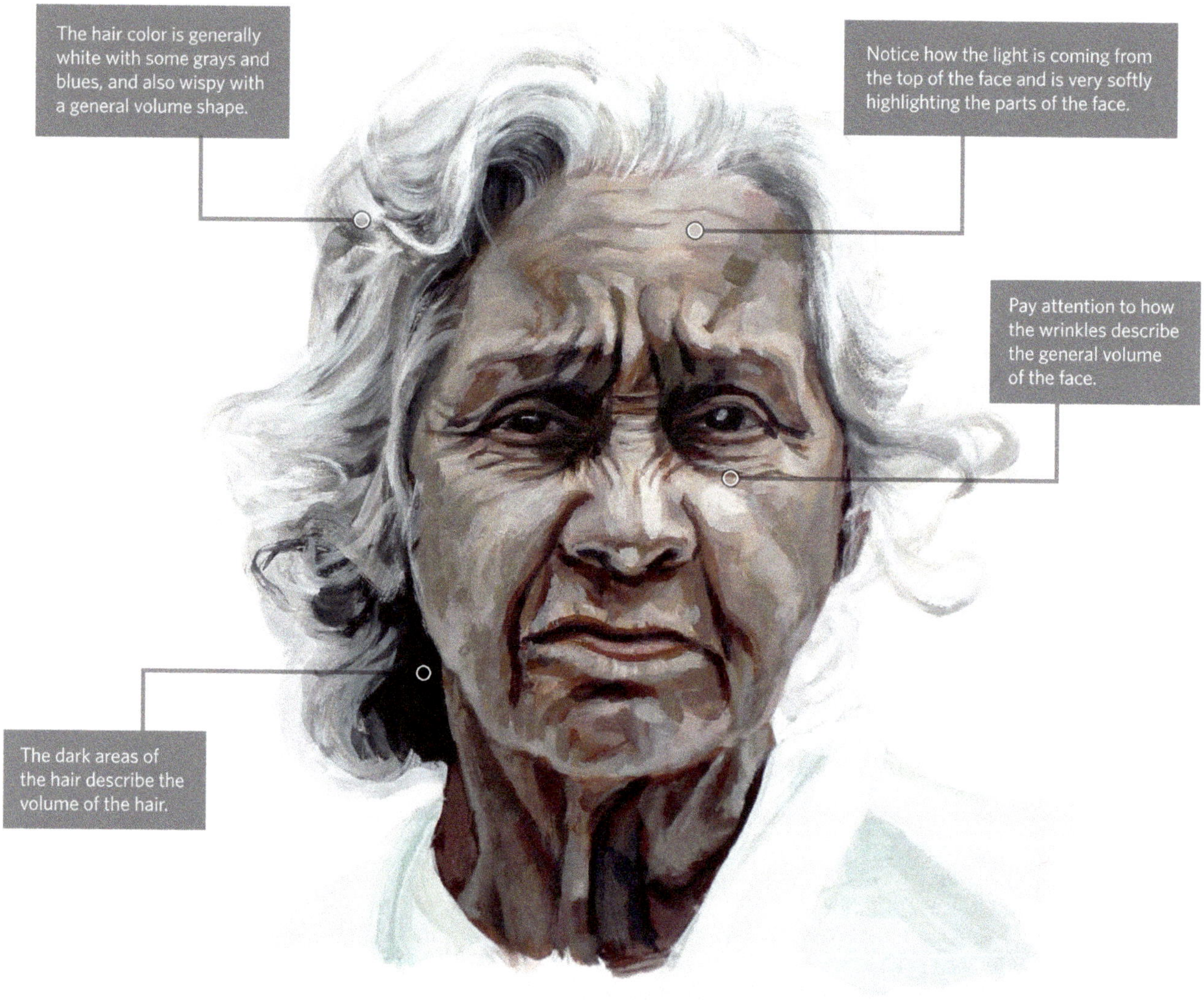

The hair color is generally white with some grays and blues, and also wispy with a general volume shape.

Notice how the light is coming from the top of the face and is very softly highlighting the parts of the face.

Pay attention to how the wrinkles describe the general volume of the face.

The dark areas of the hair describe the volume of the hair.

light red oxie
permanent red light
permanent red
cadmium red
cadmium orange
yellow ochre
permanent green
aqua teal
prussian blue
raw sienna
burnt umber
mars black
titanium white

Now try painting the elder woman yourself.

Now that you have practiced how to paint an elderly woman's face in arylic following a step-by-step tutorial, use the page on the right to try and draw from life. You can paint from the picture below, use a mirror, or ask a friend to sit for you and try different variations of compositions.

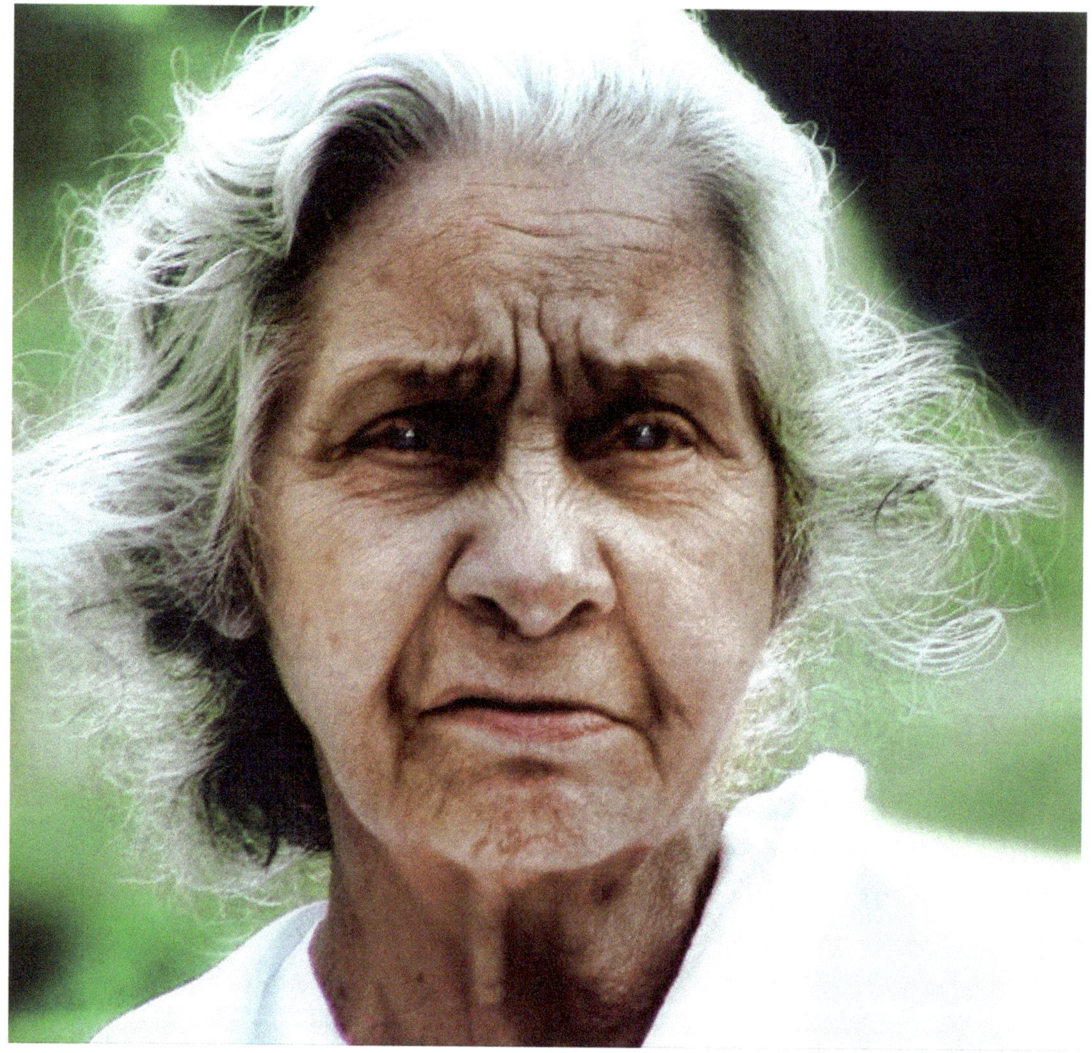

Now try painting the elder lady yourself without the grid.

Now that you have practiced different ways the face can be drawn in relation to perspective, try a couple of other perspectives. Pay attention to the shape of the facial features in different perspectives, as well as the amount of flesh visible, the lip, nose, and eyes aren't always entirely visible depending on the angle.

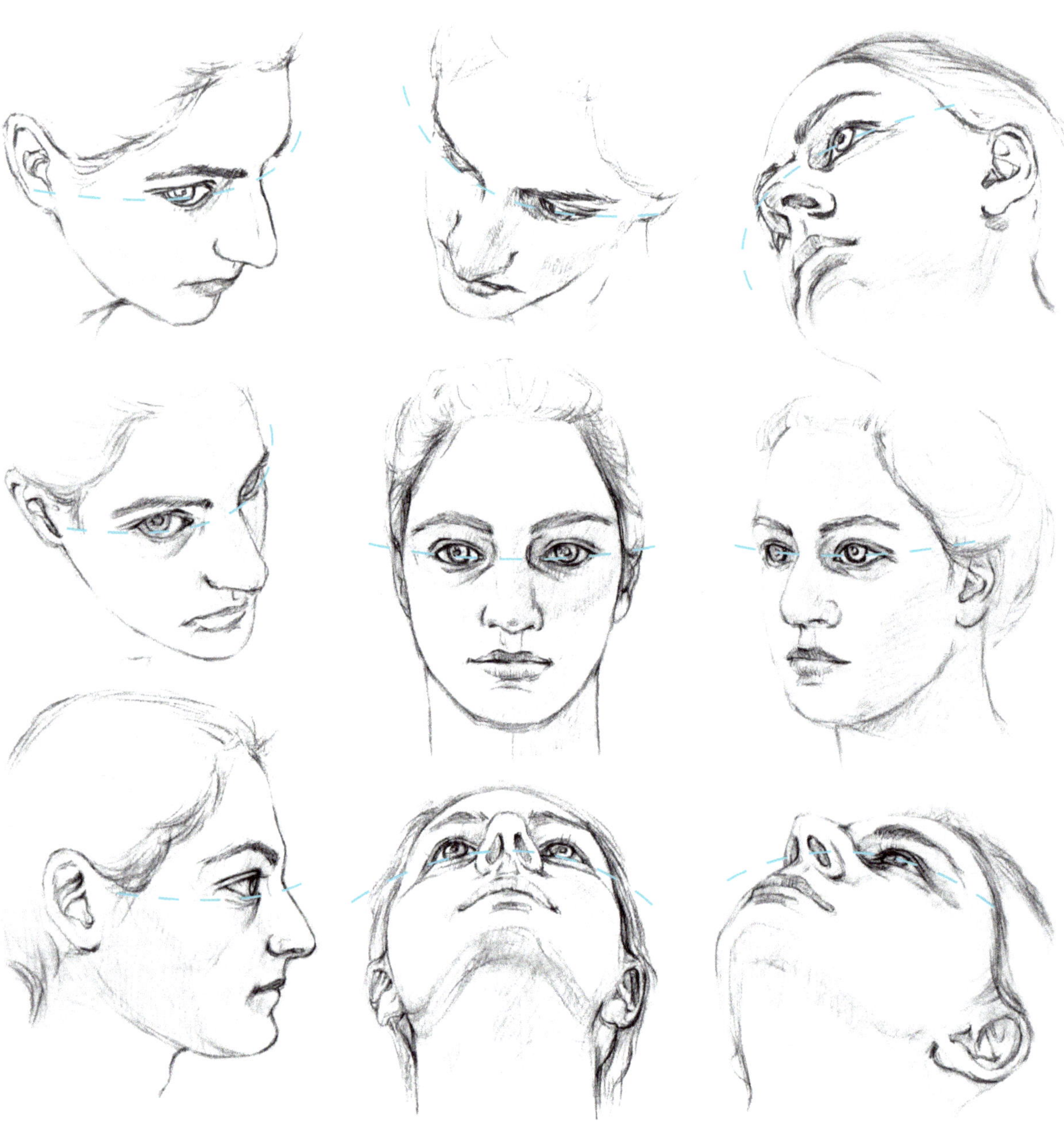

Now try drawing faces in different angles yourself.

ABOUT OOGIE HAUS

Oogie Haus is an art foundation unique for its diverse artistic endeavors, including an emphasis in art education, art & design internship opportunities, and volunteer outreach programs. There have been several book publications as well, such as "Art College Admissions," an insightful guideline for students applying to art schools.

Besides being an educational resource, Oogie Haus functions dually as an art gallery and art dealership. Through its research, it seeks to contribute a bigger network for local and international artists simultaneously curating its unique voice in todays art world. For more information please visit www.oogiehaus.com

ABOUT THE AUTHOR

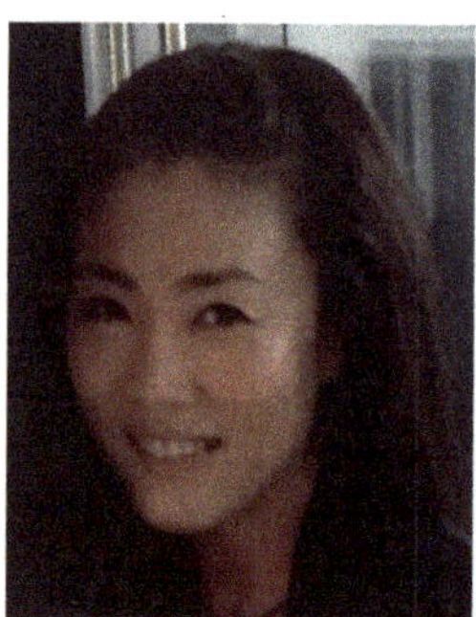

WOOK CHOI is an accomplished art dealer, education columnist, author, art educator, art gallerist, and art portfolio consultant who has guided over a thousand students to college admissions and scholarship success during the course of her 31-year teaching career.
She has received widespread recognition for her teaching methods from Mayor Michael Bloomberg; former First Lady Laura Bush; the New York Commissioner of Education, Richard P. Mills; US Congress member, Jerrold Nadler; the Alliance for Young Artists; YoungArts; and the Marie Walsh Sharpe Foundation. For more information, please visit www.wookchoi.com.

CHECK OUT SOME OF OUR OTHER BOOKS

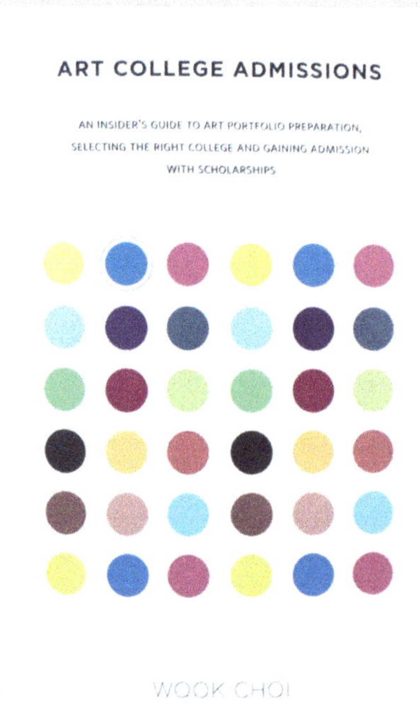

ART COLLEGE ADMISSIONS

An insider's guide to portfolio preparation, selecting the right college and gaining admission with scholarships.
In the first half of this book, you'll learn how vital a role art plays in the success of businesses today, what admissions committees at top art colleges really look for when deciding who to admit, and essential tips for developing award-winning art portfolio pieces. In the second half, you'll learn about the distinct advantages and histories of the most highly-ranked and popular art colleges in the Northeast, specific and actionable tips for getting into each school, and any changes these schools have made to their admissions criteria in recent years.

YOU CAN CONTINUE TO DEVELOP YOUR ARTISTIC SKILLS IN DIFFERENT MEDIA!

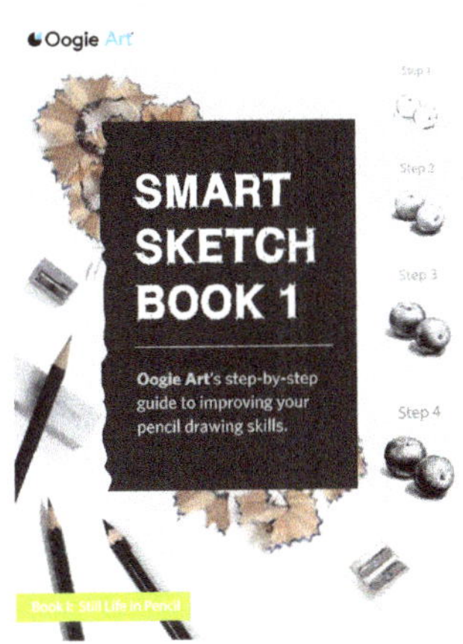

SMART SKETCHBOOK 1:
Still Life in Pencil

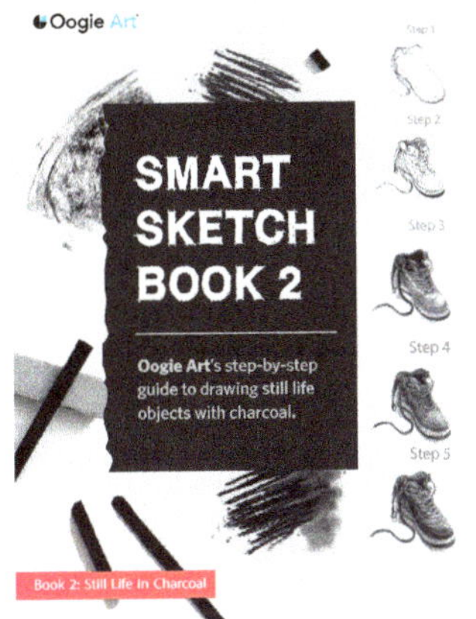

SMART SKETCHBOOK 2:
Still Life in Charcoal

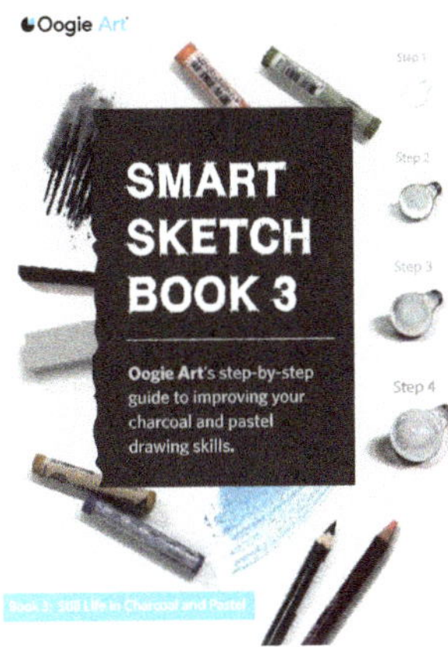

SMART SKETCHBOOK 3:
Still Life in Charcoal and Pastel

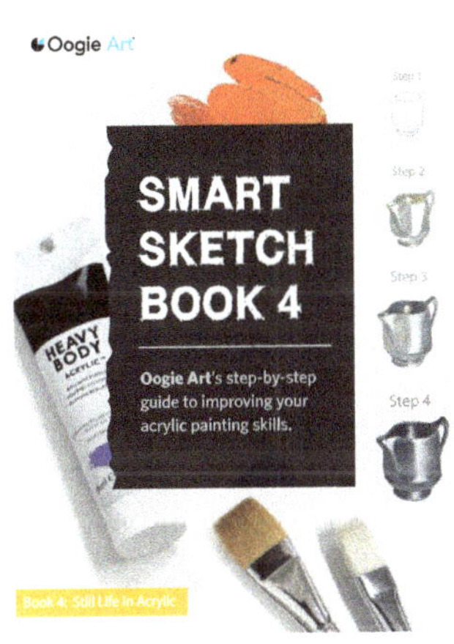

SMART SKETCHBOOK 4:
Still Life in Acrylic

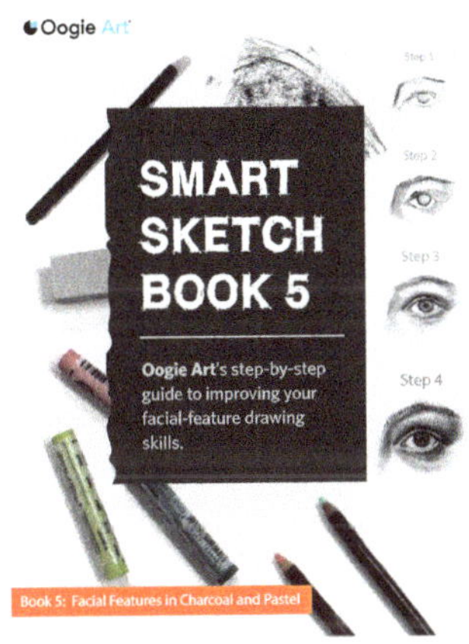

SMART SKETCHBOOK 5:
Facial Features in Charcoal and Pastel

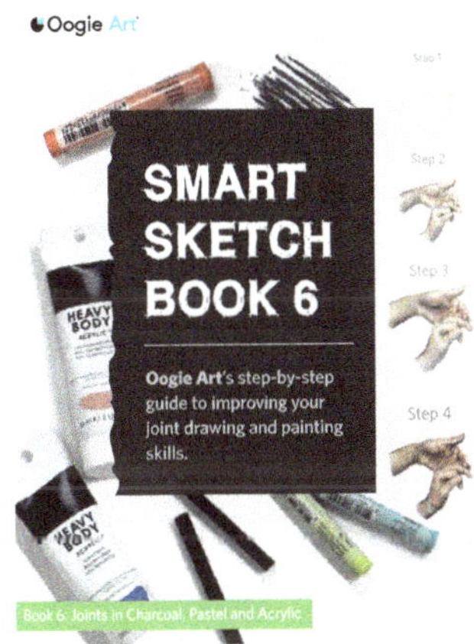

SMART SKETCHBOOK 6:
Joints in Charcoal, Pastel and Acrylic

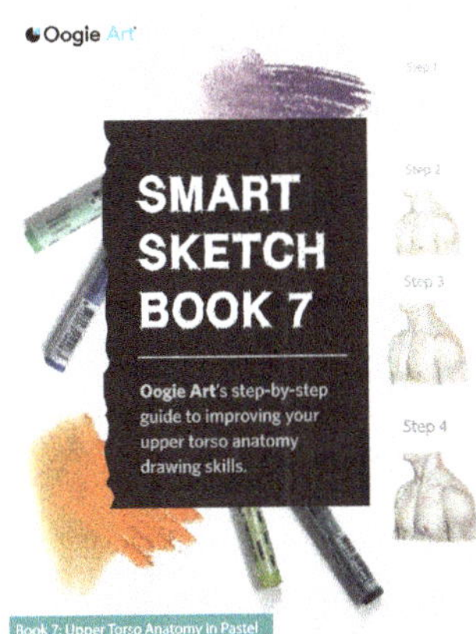

SMART SKETCHBOOK 7:
Upper Torso Anatomy in Pastel

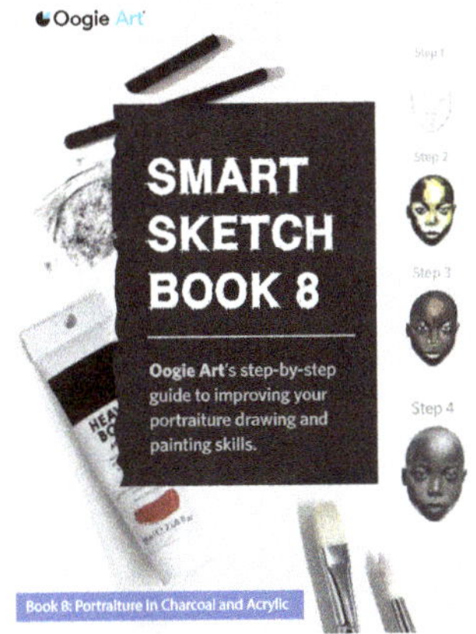

SMART SKETCHBOOK 8:
Portraiture in Charcoal and Acrylic

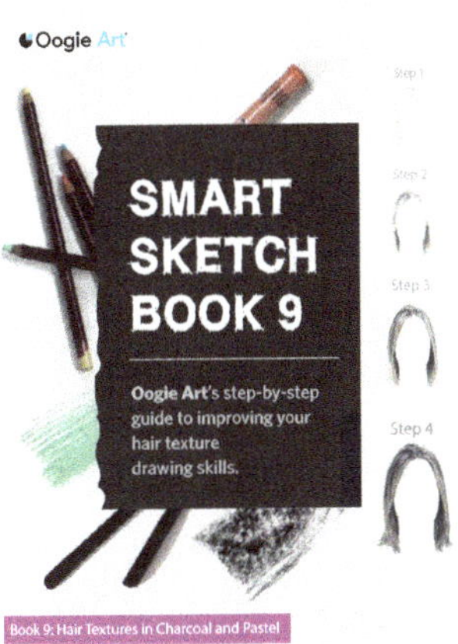

SMART SKETCHBOOK 9:
Hair Textures in Charcoal and Pastel

www.ingramcontent.com/pod-product-compliance
Ingram Content Group UK Ltd.
Pitfield, Milton Keynes, MK11 3LW, UK
UKHW062010290726
14090UKWH00022B/1486